Dedication

To my mother,

Nora Dymoke Arden,

who gave me so much help and
encouragement in my early years.

The Wheels of My Life

The Memoirs of a Dartmoor Horseman

Johnny Arden

Johnny Arden (signature)

MOORHEN PUBLISHING LLP

Published in Great Britain in 2009 by
Moorhen Publishing LLP
1 Hazelwood Close, Windmill Hill, Brixham, Devon, TQ5 9SE
www.moorhenpublishing.co.uk

A CIP catalogue record for this book is available
from the British Library.

ISBN   978-1-905856-08-4

Cover design by Deep Red Designs

Printed and bound in Great Britain by
SRP Limited, Exeter, Devon

Contents

PART 2 Dartmoor Driving 129

List of Photographs

Photographs following page 32

1. Mother, pregnant with me, winning our first race together, 1933.
2. Mid-Devon Hounds at the opening meet Chagford, 1936.
3. At age 3 planning my future from the horse's point of view.
4. Mother and Father, both mounted, with Mid-Devon Hounds, Rushford Barton, 1938.
5. Riding Jo with my cousin Buffy Knight-Bruce, 1939.
6. Major Arden in charge of the mounted Home Guard at Thornworthy Tor, 1940.
7. Stable yard at Somerford Keynes.
8. Commer lorries. The model on the left I drove for P&S, the other two are models that I drove for Oldacres. Photo courtesy of Edwin Tucker & Sons, Ashburton, Devon.
9. Early four-in-hand at Stinhall. Purpose-built waggonette with hydraulic brakes, 1979.
10. Tona Cruickshank watering in River Teign, 1982.
11. Beauty & Winnie off to Newton Abbot BFS Fair and taking customer back to the station!
12. First pony team at their first event at Osberton, 1985.
13. At Michelcombe with Tigger, 1985.
14. At Cherbourg with Debbie Ogle (a friend who was also at the event) as groom, 1986.
15. Chagford to Michelcombe drive, at the top of Bush Down in torrential rain, 1999.
16. Chagford to Michelcombe drive, turning into the East Dart Hotel for a very welcome lunch break. Pip & Dodger as leaders, Vodka & Bracken as swing, Ford & Scammel as wheelers, 1999.

Photographs following page 80

17. Ferguson T20 with belt-driven saw. Affectionately known as "the little grey fergie". Photographed at the Royal Cornwall Show.

18. Standard Fordson & Fordson Major as bought by my father and driven by me as a youngster.

19. Stationary baler of the type used when I was driving hay and straw lorries.

20. Honor & Clare with Peter in the snow.

21. Just One outside Stinhall, driven to a butt-cart, 1974.

22. Ride and drive to Fingle Bridge from Chagford, 1980.

23. Beauty with a stone roller at Chagford.

24. Beauty in the new Fenlands gig, 1982.

25. With Dutch tourists at the Walla Brook.

26. Receiving my prize from Willie Carson, Cirencester driving trials, July 1991.

27. Woolley, Bracken, Pip and Vodka (with Fiver) at Pizwell, 1990.

28. Tandem of six: Bracken, Gubbins, Woolley, Pip, Dodger & Bungle, August 1990.

29. Eight-in-hand: Gubbins & Woolley, Fingle & Pip, Dandy & Bracken, Dodger & Bungle, July 1991.

30. Maggie with Solo driven to the ralli car Christmas Day, 1991.

31. Driving Dusty to a hay rake.

32. Riding Isca using Mr Allen as packhorse to feed ponies in the snow, February 1994.

Photographs following page 144

33. Out hunting on Isca, with Rose Gaisford on Solo, winter 1996.

34. Tandem of Mr Allen & Badger at Michelcombe, 1998.

35. Ponies in the Knapp.

36. Junus.

37. Junus, who started our line of Morgans, showing the distinctive head.

38. Driving Mr Allen to a King's carriage, summer 2000.

39. Six-in-hand to Postbridge, September 2001.

40. A very steep turn onto the old A38; coach drive to Bridestowe, May 2002.

41. Lee "driving" Pip & Scammel, summer 2003.

42. Driving John Parker's Norwich Mail Coach, summer 2004.

43. Driving Victoria & Mr Allen at Scorriton Flower Show.

44. Team drive in aid of the Tsunami Disaster Appeal, March 2005.

45. Relaxing with Carolyn Owen at Michelcombe.

46. Padgent returning home after a lesson.

47. With Lee and Carolyn as groom, Padgent & Victoria in the wheel, Badger & Dusty as leaders, May 2006.

48. Victoria & Padgent, Nicki Gaisford as groom, July 2006.

Foreword

Johnny Arden is one of those special folk who not only has a passion for horses, but has also managed somehow, through thick and thin, to have made a modest living in the equine world. He was born into a Devon hunting family and has been involved with horses or ponies ever since, from racing and training to carriage driving, and everything in between.

Johnny and his family have experienced tragedy and good fortune over the last seventy years. He is both unconventional and traditional and I think his comment that he has always learnt more from when things have gone wrong, sums up his view of life ideally and is the reason he has the inventive and enthusiastic touch when he meets new challenges.

Johnny started his writing career some years ago by sharing his experiences with short tales for readers of *Carriage Driving Magazine* so it seemed the next logical step was to write his life story; the result is this intriguing book.

He is an engaging story teller with a keen sense of fun and is never afraid to laugh at himself. His love of the countryside, and in particular of Dartmoor and its hill ponies, is very evident and when coupled with his own story, which includes ingredients of drama, joy and passion taken from his store of memories, makes a fascinating and very enjoyable read.

When you have read the book and put it down you will feel that you have known Johnny all his life and can count yourself as one of his many worldwide friends.

Richard James
Editor, Carriage Driving Magazine
September 2009

Introduction

I make no claim to fame or fortune. But people tell me that my life has been unusual and that I should get my memories written down. The trouble is that I can make no claim to being a writer, either.

I was born in 1933, so those memories stretch from just before World War II up to the present day. By writing some of them down I hope to be able to record the changes I have seen in farming, working with horses, carriage driving and road haulage over the years.

It is so easy to chat about experiences while drinking a glass of whisky in front of the fire, but to try to put it into print is another thing altogether.

Today it is bitterly cold. I've seen to our horses and now I'm sitting in front of the fire – trying to cope with a laptop computer! The years have flown by. I never thought that I would get to be this age, let alone cope with these new-fangled machines.

Once I'd accepted that I was going to be too big to be a jockey, I turned my hand to other things. I have made a living by driving lots of different horses, ponies, tractors, lorries, cars and vans; riding all sorts of horses – and running a farm. Somehow, money has never stayed in my pocket.

Still, I've made lots of friends and I've had a lot of fun.

So, if you'll sit tight, I'll put to and take you for a drive through my life.

We may share some laughs and tears along the way.

Johnny Arden

PART 1

Putting To

CHAPTER 1

1933-48: Background; World War II; the disaster that was school and early farming memories

Both Mother and Father were from very well-off backgrounds. Father rose to the rank of Major during World War I and after it he also saw service in the Northwest Frontier in India. He married my mother after he retired from the army in the 1920s and then became what was called 'a gentleman farmer'.

Mother's family had strong connections with India and were large landowners in southern Ireland, but they lived at Coombe in Lustleigh where they also owned Higher Coombe.

Grandfather, on my Father's side, was the owner of a large part of Finchley, from which he derived ground rents.

So I was born into a privileged background with a silver spoon in my mouth, as they say. I am afraid that I didn't really become aware of this until much later in life, when it was too late to be of use to me. Somehow the family fortunes disappeared without me ever knowing what happened.

I had an older sister called Norah, but more generally known as Tacker. The story goes that when she was born a horse on the farm had a foal at the same time. When Mother asked a groom what the foal was like he replied, "It's a proper little tacker." This meant in Devon dialect that the foal was a really good one. So my sister was called Tacker for evermore. Tacker was ten years older than me, a gap so big that we were never really close.

I was born into this family at Stiniel, a small hamlet about two miles from Chagford, on 22nd December 1933.

In those early days Father owned a farm called Higher Stiniel together with the cottage across the road. The neighbouring farm, originally called Lower Stiniel, was owned by the Ellis Family who changed the name to Stinhall. John Ellis left Stinhall to the National Trust, but the Trust decided to sell it and Father bought it just after the war.

Of course, I have no real memory of my very early life, but I was told that I had some dangerous moments as a baby. They are incidents that give an idea of what home life was like.

Owing to a misunderstanding between Mother and my nurse I was once left outside in my pram overnight. It snowed hard that night, but apparently I was no worse for this experience.

In a drunken rage, Father threw me out of a bedroom window. My guardian angel put in a first appearance and a groom, who 'happened to be passing', caught me. The groom may well have been standing outside listening to the argument between Father and Mother, but it was lucky for me that he was there and a good catcher.

I always had a very difficult relationship with Father. His dreadful wartime experiences had left him damaged and he developed a drink problem, but he never talked to me about his problems. I didn't realise the extent of them and made no allowances. When he had been drinking the only safe thing to do was to evacuate the area. I've no idea how Mother tolerated his rages – or his chain-smoking which must have been very bad for her asthma.

Both Mother and Father really loved foxhunting, more or less to the exclusion of all else. Mother was an expert horsewoman who rode in, and indeed won, a number of point-to-point races – some while she was expecting me. When I went on to become a jockey it amused me to think that not many jockeys can claim to have ridden winners before they were born!

My parents were the prime movers in managing to restart the Mid-Devon Hounds in 1936. This pack had ceased for the First World War and the country had been taken over by the South Devon Hunt, who were very reluctant to hand it back. After a great struggle, they were allowed to restart hunting again following a ruling by the Masters of Foxhounds Association in January 1937. At first they were known as the Cranmere Harriers. Sir Raleigh Phillpotts was one of the main movers in this effort.

Of course, I was far too young to be involved in any of this, or even to have been aware of it, but even after all these years I still meet some elderly people who have a go at me about it.

When the hunt restarted, Mother acted as whipper-in. Was she the first female whipper-in in the country?

There is a building in the yard at Higher Stiniel that had been an old cottage. It fell down one Christmas Eve, so father had it rebuilt as a cowshed. I can just remember Stones, the builders, doing this. Father later turned it into hunt kennels and had a large steel-railed run built behind it for the hounds.

Mr Bert Rice and his family lived in the old cottage across the road. Father's only bit of modernisation was to fit a cold water tap. There was only an earth closet – a common feature at that time.

Father installed a Lister generator before the war. It was a petrol model that had to be started by swinging a big handle and it could be a bit tricky to start. The generator charged a row of glass batteries that provided electric light for the house. Father put the generator into an old, thatched roundhouse that had been used as part of the threshing barn. The horses used to walk round and round pulling a gearing that had a large wooden pole in the middle of the roundhouse. This was connected to a row of cogs right around the outside that made the power to drive the thresher in the barn beside it.

Owing to the lack of petrol during the war, the generator fell into disuse and we had to manage with paraffin lights throughout the war.

*

At the outbreak of war my parents employed at least two maids in the house, a full-time groom called Mr Ward, Tom Bunch as kennel huntsman and a couple of farm labourers. All this on less than one hundred acres! This wasn't at all unusual in those days.

The war changed everything. Mother and Father were soon running it all themselves. Tom Bunch, like Father, had served in the first war and was too old to be called up, but he left to hunt the South Berkshire Hunt for the duration of the war.

I really missed having his son, Gordon, to play with. However, Gordon (also known as Bunchy) came to stay for some of the time.

19

I presume that all the others were called up for war service.

The farm had to change from a purely grass farm. Arable crops, dairy cows, chickens were the order of the day. A small steep field at the back of the farm was turned into a market garden.

Bunchy and I built a pillbox out of scrap wood and old galvanised iron in the middle of that garden. It had a fine view over the hamlet. We fought many imaginary battles with the Germans from here. Of course we always won!

The Home Guard was being formed. I think they were called the Local Defence Volunteers, LDV for short, at the beginning. Father was put in charge of a mounted company formed to patrol our side of Dartmoor. They were based at Kestor, high on the moor, where they had stabling and a timber hut. At first they didn't have army guns, so the late Sir Raleigh Phillpotts personally provided them with deer-stalking rifles.

I remember that on several occasions the Home Guard and the Army held manoeuvres on the farm. Bunchy and I were used as messenger boys. A soldier once jumped out of the hedge with his rifle to stop us. I was so frightened that I had an embarrassing accident.

I watched quite a lot of the training. I was taught to fire an old Winchester rifle at the age of six, and became quite a good shot. On one training exercise the Home Guard had to ambush some regular soldiers, who had Bren gun carriers. Father got his men to partially cut down a tree. When the soldiers came down the road into a granite cutting, the Home Guard dropped the tree across the road trapping the regular soldiers, and then he had another tree dropped behind them. The umpires said the Home Guard had won – what excitement there was!

My parents gave parties for the soldiers that were based in Chagford. One night they fired champagne corks up the stairs. I thought that the Germans had arrived. They certainly frightened me. I believe that they were from The Warwickshire Yeomanry. The name Cadbury springs to mind – I think he was an officer.

I can quite clearly remember German bombers going overhead to bomb Exeter and Plymouth. That awful droning of their engines and the noise of the bombs exploding will be with me all my life. I remember watching them going over in the night sky; the searchlights making patterns and the roar of the anti-aircraft guns that could be heard quite clearly, even though we were more than twenty miles from either place. The night sky glowed as the cities burned.

Father said that the hall in our old granite farmhouse was going to be the safest place to shelter during raids. One night, when the noise of the bombing died off, Father said it was all over. He just made it to the top of the stairs when there was a terrific series of explosions. Father came back down the stairs in one big leap. We all shot back into our hiding places. When we went outside next morning there was a line of bomb craters right across the farm.

One night Mother had a telephone call from army headquarters. They had received reports that Germans had landed on Dartmoor and asked Mother to take a message to Father who was patrolling the moor on horseback with his mounted Home Guard. She collected a neighbouring farmer with his shotgun and set off for the moor in her Singer sports car to the Warren House Inn, which is the third highest pub in England. She had a feeling that the Home Guard would be there – I wonder why? At the top of Bush Down they saw some grey objects crawling along the side of the road. Of course they had no headlights because of the blackout, but they were both certain that they had found the Germans. Mother changed down a gear and crept up behind them until they were as close as they dared go. Then she quickly turned the car round, while the farmer fired at the Germans as fast as he could. What luck! They seemed to have caught them unawares, because there was no answering fire. But they didn't wait to find out and dashed back home in a panic. Father was still out: maybe he had found some more of the invasion force? Eventually he and his cavalry came home after a good night at the Warren House Inn. No, they hadn't seen or heard of any invading Germans. All was quiet so they went off to bed, hoping that there wouldn't be any trouble during the night. Morning came and everything still seemed quiet, but just to make sure Father went to Bush Down to check. All he found was a couple of dead sheep beside the road.

Growing up in wartime meant that I had to do many things

around the farm and kennels that were normally the jobs of grown-ups, including whipping-in to hounds. Mother's health was bad and all the men had gone to war, so I had to help. I spent a lot of the winter mucking out, fetching back knackers (animals that had died on the farms) for the hounds, and skinning carcasses. It was all part of the job that needed doing, and I thought nothing of it: a far cry from today when children are barely allowed to feed the chickens!

I worked horses on the farm, milked the cows by hand and learned to drive the Standard Fordson tractor (one of the first in the parish). It was a TVO engine, which meant that it started on petrol (which was on ration), and when it got hot enough you turned a tap and it ran on TVO, a type of paraffin. If you forgot to change over, it stopped as the petrol tank was small, and if you were unlucky it wouldn't start again. Then you would have to walk home and hope there was some more petrol there. The tractor was started with a handle that was very heavy to swing. If you had your thumb around it and it kicked back on you it could break your thumb; if you let it tick over for too long the plugs would oil up and you would have to take them out. You could test for the offending plug by putting a screwdriver on each and listening for the change in engine note, but if you let it touch the wrong bits you got a terrific shock. What a caper it all seems looking back.

Thank goodness for modern diesels. But they were still a long way in the future as far as we were concerned, and when the Fordson was going well I thought I was king of the field, roaring up and down. What a noise! But if Father was home I was left to work Rosy, the cart mare (I'd never heard of shire horses). If a pair of horses was needed, we used to put a hunter in beside her. This was great fun as we often started off a bit lively, but the hunter soon got tired from pulling the harrows and settled down.

Later on when the Americans were in the war, we children were playing in the River Teign when a big American truck came roaring down the lane and got stuck on the old stone bridge. There are lots of these bridges on Dartmoor, built hundreds of years ago and wide enough to carry pack ponies, which were the most common form of transport in those days, but modern transport can have problems. Not for this soldier! He jumped out of the cab and knocked the mudguards off the lorry with an axe. He slung them in the river and went on his way.

Just before the Normandy invasion we had some American soldiers camped on Stiniel Down. They had bows and arrows, and could hit anything they aimed at; whether they were a special unit or just having fun we never found out. We kids were convinced that they were Red Indians and we were always rather surprised that they didn't scalp us. Instead they gave us lots of candy and gum, which was fantastic as those luxuries were strictly rationed.

Much of the work was still being done by hand, as it had always been done. During the war, and just after, there was a great shortage of labour. We used to have some help from the Land Army girls. I was too young for them to interest me. They certainly were a great help. They were brought to the farm in a lorry.

We also had German and Italian POWs who drained some marshy fields. I was very frightened of them to begin with. One of them pointed his shovel at me from the ditch he was digging and shouted, "Bang! Bang!" He really managed to frighten me, but they were great fun once we got to know them.

One of them turned out to be a good horseman. He was called Fritz, of course, and he stayed on with Father for some time after the war.

It is only thinking about it now that I realise how hard everybody worked during this wartime period.

Mother must have found it very difficult as she had been brought up in a world with maids, gardeners and grooms. There were none of the modern things such as fridges, vacuum cleaners or washing machines – not even electricity. Cooking was on an old black iron range, but as coal was rationed she had to do a lot of cooking on an open fire or oil stove.

She also helped as a whipper-in to my Father, helping him to hunt the foxhounds. Hunting was allowed to continue as it was seen as essential pest control, although the best horses were commandeered by the Army at the start of the war. I think there was even an official ration of grain for hunting horses that remained.

Very often Mother drove the tractor to collect the knackers for the kennels. All this must have been very hard for her, as she had been brought up as a lady.

She suffered badly from asthma and got pneumonia twice. She also had to cope with Father's drink problem. I will never understand how she coped with all these difficulties.

Owing to Mother's illness, I often had to help Father hunt the hounds. I became a whipper-in at about ten years old. I was considered too young to wear a pink coat. Petrol rationing meant that we had to ride to all the meets and, harder still, had to ride home again, often in the dark. In memory it always seemed to be raining. I can feel myself back there now: cold, wet, tired, hungry and with sparks flying from the horses' hooves.

I felt very important riding along behind Father and his hounds. Only very few people were able to come out hunting during the war: just a few local farmers and maybe a serviceman on leave.

One day around this time we were out hunting and on the way home Father called in at a farm, ending up getting very drunk. Father and the farmer fell asleep in the hay. The hounds began to chase the chickens. The farmer's wife got a bit excited about this and angrily told me to take the hounds home. I got on to my pony, Misty, but the hounds wouldn't leave Father. I climbed onto Father's horse, called The Old Mare. She had a mouth of iron and shot off towards home – at least I hoped she was going the right way. The stirrup leathers were much too long for me. In wartime there were no signposts and I was miles from anywhere I knew. However, the hounds did follow the mare. After many miles we hit a main road and just as we got onto it a convoy of enormous lorries, full of black American soldiers, started to pass us. The last one stopped and they asked me where I was going with my hound dogs in the dark. They were very kind and gave me a huge chunk of chocolate.

In the end, The Old Mare brought hounds and me safely home. In fact, she trotted straight into her stable, nearly knocking my head off on the door frame.

I don't think Father's life was worth living for a few days after Mother had finished with him.

Father and I were out hunting on Dartmoor one day, when all of a sudden we heard shells whistling over us. We could see the American gunners on the top of the next hill. Father shouted at me to stay with him and set off at full gallop straight towards the guns. I thought this was great fun, although in hindsight it was terribly dangerous as we could easily have been killed. When we reached the guns, Father shouted at the officer in charge, giving him a right dressing-down for firing his guns while hounds were out working, and then he set about him with his hunting crop, much to the delight of the soldiers. Then we collected the hounds up and went and looked for a fox, as if nothing had happened.

There were always shells lying about and we would very often hear them clink on the horses hooves as we galloped across the moor. But the slit trenches were the most dangerous things; when the bracken and heather grew over them, they were very difficult to see. Mother had a bad tumble when her horse fell after putting a foot in one. There was no air ambulance in those days, and we were too far from the road for a motor ambulance to reach her, so we had to improvise. Luckily we were not too far from some fields, so we borrowed a gate from an empty one. We lifted it off its hinges and used it as an improvised stretcher to carry Mother back to the road. Someone had ridden on to a farmhouse where we knew that there was a telephone and rang for an ambulance which met us and took Mother on to hospital.

One evening I had to look for some lost hounds in the Fingle Valley. I got completely lost, but came across some people who were charcoal burning. I thought that I was saved. Not at all – they were all foreigners who didn't speak English, so they were no help. I eventually found the Hunter's Path up the valley. It had been neglected for a long time and the gorse had grown out over the path. As a result my pony Misty kept going out towards the edge. There is a tremendous drop down to the River Teign and we nearly went over. My God, I was so frightened and crying! Wasn't I glad to hear Father's hunting horn away in front of me!

Mother had to move into a flat in Exeter for a short time to be near the hospital for treatment. I spent some of my school holidays there. One morning I saw a single-engined plane coming straight at our house. There was a terrific explosion. When I picked myself up from the floor I could see bullet holes in the wall behind me. The house next door had been completely flattened.

I could never remember the address of that property, but recently I saw an advertisement for a house for sale in Barings Close and recognised it. I went along to see it one day and sure enough it was the same house, but now a new house stands beside it. Nowadays there is a well-laid-out garden in front of it. In my time there it was a derelict space with a bomb shelter in the middle. That was the closest that I came to being killed during the war. Yet another lucky escape.

I was a member of the Mid Devon Pony Club just after the war. We all had a lot of fun. There wasn't too much instruction, but we had fun playing gymkhana games and other games when the adults weren't watching. The girls outnumbered the boys, which suited me well. I had almost no chance of meeting girls, as the farm was pretty remote in those days.

We had a club camp at Yelfords outside Chagford. For some reason it was a joint camp with the Silverton Hunt PC. A Sergeant Williams of the King's Troop came as an instructor with his horse Nuthatch. I was to meet Nuthatch later at Melton Mowbray when I did my army service. The sergeant was a good instructor and helped us all.

This camp marked my meeting lots of girls for the first time. What an experience it was to be. We were all sleeping in lofts and barns at different addresses. There was a lot of night walking going on. Cigarettes and some booze were brought in – all very daring and naughty in those days. I still meet some of this crowd and we have a good laugh about it all. I wasn't allowed to go to another camp!

*

I disliked school from the beginning. As the years passed, I disliked it more.

I was first sent as a day boy to a private junior school at Meldon Hall, but I soon changed to another school at a large house called Holy Street Manor. There was an old watermill at the rear of it. Our school was in the loft above the very grand stables. I was having great difficulty in learning to read and I never have been any good at doing arithmetic. Perhaps I was dyslexic, but I don't think anybody knew about that condition back then.

I made friends with a girl who was a boarder at the school. I remember her as being very unhappy. I'm not sure why, but I think she may have just lost her parents. I asked Mother if she could come and play at home during the weekend. We were both about six years old at the time. She came and we spent a couple of happy days playing around the farm. I remember that we played with the foxhounds through the bars of the kennels.

I eventually moved on to another school and I never saw her again – until recently. A couple came down to us in Michelcombe for a holiday carriage drive out across the moor, and they brought Mother with them. Badger and Mr Allen, two of our cobs, had given us a lovely drive and after making them comfortable in their stables we all went indoors for a cup of tea.

During the drive I hadn't had the opportunity to talk to Mother very much, as she was sitting in the back of the carriage and I was concentrating on driving the horses, but sitting around the table I was able to chat to them all.

When I told them that I was brought up in Chagford, the mother said, "I remember Chagford. I was evacuated there during the War. I remember a little boy at the school invited me back home to his farm one weekend. I was quite young at the time," she said thoughtfully, "but I seem to remember playing with some foxhounds through the bars of their kennel."

It took a minute for this to sink in, but slowly we pieced our stories together and realised that she was the little girl that I had taken pity on. She now lives in the London area with her family, but what a strange coincidence after nearly seventy years.

As my schooling was not proving very successful I was sent to a preparatory boarding school at Okehampton. I must have been about eight years old. I was very homesick and hated every minute of it.

There were two other boys who couldn't spell, so we were all taught by an old lady in a special class. She had great success with the spelling, but I was hopeless at arithmetic too, and at this school it was taught by the headmaster who seemed to take great delight in beating me at every possible opportunity. Today any teacher doing what he did would end up in prison. I never found out why he seemed to hate me so much.

All the boys had numbers. Very recently a man phoned me to ask if I was the Arden who was number 34 at this school. He had been number 31. Sad to say I didn't remember him. He reminded me that I had taken a group of pupils home to Father's farm as a treat. We'd had a puncture on the way back, so we were late returning to school. I got another beating, although it was hardly my fault.

The headmaster's wife, who was a kindly old soul, let me help on their small farm. I drove the working horses and milked the cows. I now realise that she was keeping me away from her husband. There was never any sexual bother; he just took every excuse to give me a good hiding.

Writing this has brought back a host of memories of this part of my life. We all had to wear corduroy shorts, as did most small boys in those days.

One winter we had a blizzard. As we didn't have any long trousers I suffered from huge chilblains on my knees. I also got them on my ears. Heating was almost non-existent in the whole school. Coal was in short supply because of the war and we had to do working parties in a wood owned by the school to fetch logs to keep the fires going. We pulled a scout cart that had wooden wheels and a handle to steer it by. To pull it along we had two long ropes attached to the hubs of the wheels.

During this blizzard the school ran out of food. We had to pull the cart for several miles in deep snow, including up a very steep hill, to reach the Southern Railway station at Okehampton where a train loaded with supplies was waiting for us. This meant that we had to pull a fully-loaded cart back to school still in our shorts.

Every winter the dormitories were freezing cold. We had to

wash in cold water that often had ice on it.

Being wartime there was a large military camp right beside our playing field. Polish Navy sailors were billeted there for some time. Then there were a lot of American soldiers stationed there. They were the first black men I had ever seen. They gave us candy, which was marvellous, as sweets were rationed here, so we thought they were great guys! Our headmaster became aware of this and we were forbidden to accept the candy. We still kept taking it at every opportunity, but had to keep it hidden or swallow it quickly. They also showed us baseball.

The Americans had huge lorries. One day a Sherman tank ran off the road and ended up in the school grounds.

The camp was always busy: lorries and tanks coming and going, soldiers on exercises and a general air of ordered activity. Then, suddenly, one morning they were gone. The previous evening had been as busy as ever, now it was all shut up and silent. We kids were very disappointed that our friends had left without even saying goodbye, but of course we had no idea that they had left for D-Day.

We had to learn all the different types of aeroplanes so that we could spot which ones were ours.

A few other memories spring to mind. Some of us had riding lessons with a lady who had a few ponies. I used to enjoy this, of course. Very occasionally we were marched to the town cinema in crocodile fashion to see a film. One of the dormitories had a fire escape that we used to go midnight swimming in the school open-air pool. This was very daring and naughty, but we never got caught.

Doubtless our parents were all paying handsomely for us to enjoy this Spartan existence. Certainly I have never had such a tough time in my life. Even military service was a doddle compared to this.

Whatever they were paying, it didn't work and I failed my common entrance exam for Sherborne College. I was sent instead to Dean Close at Cheltenham. This was a very religious boarding school. It had a grand chapel. We did lots of praying!

I was still not very successful. By now I just hated school and had no confidence. I was convinced that I was just plain stupid.

I was put into a class of no-hopers. We had no special teaching to help us. We were definitely not getting anywhere. In the winter we played rugger and I really got to like this. In the spring we had to play hockey. One of the masters had played for England, so great importance was placed on it, but I much preferred rugger.

The cane was still in regular use. Even the prefects were allowed to use this punishment. I always seemed to get more than my fair share, so nothing much changed.

I had to travel on the steam train from Exeter to Cheltenham and I enjoyed the journey. I used to get cinders in my eyes from looking out of the windows.

Trains passed right beside the school. There was a branch line that left the main line right outside the school. I believe it went to Kingham. We spent a lot of time collecting engine numbers.

We had to wear mortarboards on our heads. I thought that we looked quite ridiculous.

One day I followed some older boys who were visiting a Welsh housemaid who lodged in the school. Guess who got caught! The others all ran away! Another beating followed and I was told that my presence was no longer needed at this school.

I was nearly fifteen, so that was the end of school. I was delighted.

*

As I said previously, whenever I was home from school I helped with both the farming and the hunting, often doing adult jobs at a very young age.

Farm work continued with the ever-changing seasons.

Hay-making was a fun time. We worked the horses turning the hay and sweeping it to the rick with a wooden hay sweep. A horse pulled a wooden bar that had teeth sticking out in front to collect the hay. I would run along behind holding the handles, trying to keep it all level while steering Rosy, the old cart mare, towards the rick where I had to heave the handles upwards, turning it all over to leave the hay beside the rick. As Rosy couldn't do it all, the hunters were put to pulling rakes and the turner which had forks at the back that were driven by the wheels of the machine. If a horse ran away you couldn't jump over the back as the forks would catch you. It was a noisy machine and I had more than one trip going very fast!

We had a haypole, a type of crane that lifted the hay on to the rick. A horse was hitched to a wire hawser which was hooked to a spring-loaded grab. It took one of us to lead the horse, the other handled the grab. One time when I was leading the horse my friend Bunchy was working the grab when his leg got caught in it. He yelled out, the horse shot off and Bunchy was left hanging in the sky.

We sometimes used a pony to tramp the rick down tight. When the rick was nearly full he was pushed off onto a heap of hay on the ground.

Mother used to bring tea up to the field. Home-made scones, proper clotted cream and home-made jam. Mother used to make clotted cream by cooking milk, very slowly on the ashes. She also made butter and cheese. What may be nowadays regarded as a luxury was then, because it was all home-produced and off-ration, the cheapest food around.

Another thing I remember was that a wireless powered by an accumulator (a type of battery) was always put on a table in the corner of the field, and someone had to listen all the time in case the Germans invaded. Shotguns, rifles and a revolver of Father's of First World War vintage were also stacked by the table.

After hay-making came the corn harvest and this was all a long time before combine harvesters. We used to have to cut around the outside of the field by hand with a scythe before we could start using the binder, which was pulled by three carthorses. It had a moving knife, and above this were sails, which swept the crop onto a series of moving canvas conveyor belts and then through a mechanical knotter that finally threw out a sheaf – a bundle of straw with the ears of corn still on it.

We had to stand these sheaves up together and make stitches, or stooks, set on the binder drive wheel marks. As I remember, they had to stand for three Sundays before being harvested – I wonder if we ever get three weeks dry weather nowadays!

Remember, the binder was also land-wheel driven, so it

was hard for horses to pull. After the sheaves had ripened and dried, we had to take the stitches apart and throw them down with the butt ends towards the sun and wind to dry a bit more. Then we brought the horses and wagons along, and loaded them up, putting the butts to the outside on both sides, and then filling the centre with sheaves placed alternately, making sure that the load was kept straight and upright. Not too easy if you were loading on the side of a hill, which we were nearly always doing.

These wagons didn't have brakes, so the horses had to stop them with britching, a strap around their hindquarters that they "sat" on going downhill. If the hill was very steep we'd put a dragshoe under the back wheel; this was a little 'sledge' that stopped the wheel going round. It worked well if the road was a gravel surface, but on tarmac it had the reverse effect. I once tried to go down a very steep hill. I had been told to go the long way around which wasn't so steep, but of course I knew better. The wagon ran away down the hill, pushing Rosy in front of it, with a very frightened little boy on the top of the load – although I was supposed to be leading her. I got away with it, but never tried that trick again.

The corn was made into circular ricks, each standing on a bed made from hedge trimmings. When the ricks were made they were thatched using rushes that we had cut with a scythe in a boggy field, and tied up into bundles. The thatch was secured with spars from hazel or willow. This was a real work of art and had to be 'just proper' so that the rain wouldn't get in.

Rushes were also used to make potato caves to store potatoes over the winter.

Little did any of us realise that we were seeing the last of harvests using horses before the tractors took over. From then on a totally new way of farming would develop.

As soon as corn harvest was over we started getting the hunters fit, ready for the start of the hunting season. Even though they were being used for mounted Home Guard duties and as harness horses both on the road and farm, they still had to be fit enough to gallop across open moorland.

I remember Father having a very fast and strong trotting pony that pulled an American four-wheel buggy. We used to go

1 Mother, pregnant with me, winning our first race together, 1933.

2 Mid-Devon Hounds at the opening meet Chagford, 1936

3 At age 3 planning my future from the horse's point of view.

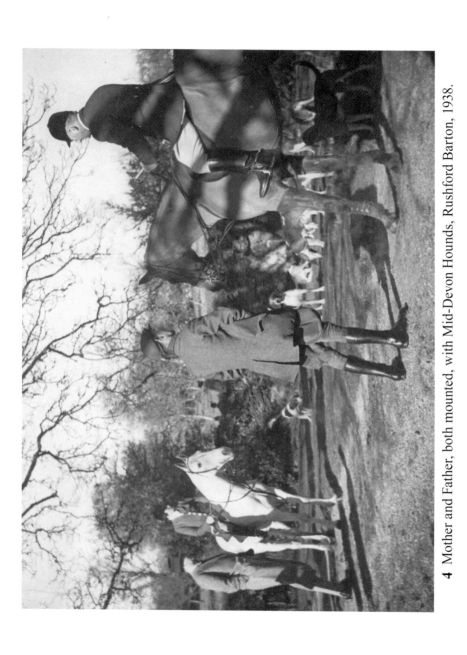

4 Mother and Father, both mounted, with Mid-Devon Hounds, Rushford Barton, 1938.

5 Riding Jo with my cousin Buffy Knight-Bruce, 1939.

6 Major Arden in charge of the mounted Home Guard at Thornworthy Tor, 1940.

7 Stable yard at Somerford Keynes.

8 Commer lorries. The model on the left I drove for P&S, the other two are models that I drove for Oldacres. Photo courtesy of Edwin Tucker & Sons, Ashburton, Devon.

9 Early four-in-hand in Stinhall. Purpose-built waggonette with hydraulic brakes, 1979.

10 Tona Cruickshank watering in River Teign, 1982.

11 Beauty & Winnie off to Newton Abbot BFS Fair and
taking a customer back to the station!

12 First pony team at their first event at Osberton, 1985.

13 At Michelcombe with Tigger, 1985.

14 At Cherbourg with Debbie Ogle (a friend who was also
at the event) as groom, 1986.

15 Chagford to Michelcombe drive, at the top of Bush Down in torrential rain, 1999.

16 Chagford to Michelcombe drive, turning into the East Dart Hotel for a very welcome lunch break. Pip & Dodger as leaders, Vodka & Bracken as swing, Ford & Scammel as wheelers, 1999.

to Grandfather's big house beside the sea at Torquay with this pony. We'd leave very early in the morning to avoid the heat of the day, spend the day beside the sea, and then come home in the evening. It must have been over twenty miles each way.

There was always plenty of work on the farm, apart from harvesting. I very often worked with Bunchy, who was older than me, and therefore could work faster. He was good at most things, but he excelled at hoeing, and won every race we had up and down the fields of mangles. I hated hoeing! It's much too slow for me, and I hated losing every time.

Still, all that practice came in useful a few years later. I was driving a hay and straw lorry on the Cotswolds when I saw a gang of men hoeing a field, and they didn't look very fast. I had a bit of time to kill, so I pulled up and somewhat rashly bet the best man a fiver that I could do a row faster than him. A basic wage was only ten pounds a week in those days. He looked at me, obviously wondering why a lorry driver should pull up and make a challenge like that, but I expect he thought the odds were too much in his favour to refuse the challenge.

"You're on," he said, throwing me a spare hoe – and we were off.

Within a few yards I was slightly ahead of him, and by the end of the row I had left him way behind. His mates shouted and cheered, but he wasn't too happy. There was a lot of muttering, but he kept his word and handed over the fiver. I thanked him, jumped into my lorry and roared off, no doubt leaving them wondering how a lorry driver had beaten them at their own job!

Those were the days before myxomotosis and rabbits would do tremendous damage to cornfields. As the corn was being cut they retreated into the last bit standing and it was the youngsters' job to run after them and kill them with sticks. With strict food rationing in force, rabbit made a welcome addition to the meat ration. A trapper would pay a farmer a lot of money for the rights to trap on the farm, or to use ferrets and nets. The weekly bus to Newton Abbot was always loaded with rabbits and every other thing that could be sold in the market.

We always kept South Devon cows – the ones with big horns! Cows have never been my favourite animals. When TT testing was introduced just after the war we had a really difficult job on our hands; we didn't have a cattle crush and many of the bullocks were three or four years old and as wild as hawks.

Thinking of vets, we once had a cow that couldn't get up. Father called the vet out, but even he couldn't find what the matter was. They were discussing what to do when old Dick came along. Dick had worked on the farm for years, and also helped us with the horses and hounds.

"You silly lot," he said, "a cow doesn't get up like a horse with its legs out in front like that. Us'll have to tuck her legs back under her." Sure enough, up she came. Father and the vet beat a hasty retreat indoors.

Calving sometimes presented problems. Why did the cows so often calve at night and usually under a bank across the other side of the farm? We didn't have mains electricity at the farm. The house had a generator to give us lights and power, but that didn't go as far as the barns where we had to rely on oil lanterns. I remember one young cow that was getting into trouble giving birth to her first calf. We had managed to get her into a loose box in the barn, but things were still not going well for her. I was just opening the door to go in to try to help her, when she spun round and charged across the box towards me. I just managed to get out and shut the door in time.

Time to get help, I thought and went off to get Father from the stables, where he was doing the horses up ready for the night. He came with me back to the cow.

"What's the matter with you, Johnny? Just go into her box and do as I told you…"

He hadn't even got as far as opening the door when the cow saw him and with a terrific bellow she charged. The door flew off its hinges, flattening Father into the gutter and the mud. I shot up the ladder into the loft a bit sharpish as the cow trotted out into the yard. Father extricated himself from under the door, cursing and spitting mud and went off to find some of the other men to help. When the coast was clear I came down from the loft and found myself a safer job out of sight. Two strong men came back with Father and they soon had the cow back in her box. That extra bit of exercise must have done the trick; we soon had a healthy calf with a proud mum.

34

Father was an early riser, even when he had been very much the worse for wear the night before. So we fed the horses, milked half-a-dozen cows by hand and did all the mucking out before we went in for breakfast. Farmers' sons didn't earn any wages in those days, so if some money came our way we were very lucky.

We were still milking by hand and the cows always seemed to be able to wrap their mucky tails around my head or put their foot in the bucket or kick me into the gutter. After we had cooled the milk by putting the churns into a stream, we pulled them up to the milk stand (a platform at lorry height), on a little four-wheeled wagon made of wood, with a handle back to the fifth jockey wheel. We used to ride on it down the hill back to the farm, and steer it with the handle pulled back over. Of course, there were no brakes, but there wasn't much chance of meeting a car in those days.

About 1944 we had a picnic by the river close to Gidleigh; my sister was there with her baby. One of us stepped onto a wasp's nest and panic reigned as we all tried to get away from the wasps. This was on the site of a civil war battle in a field called Bloody Meadow – I think we called it something similar!

I've just remembered something I haven't thought about for many years. Mother used to hide Easter eggs in a little wood we had on the farm. What fun we had trying to find those eggs.

Collecting knackers to feed the hounds resulted in some funny incidents.

Dick Perrot worked for Father. He was a tall, gaunt man, who was kind and very laid back about life. He used to drive the knacker lorry, which was an old pre-war Bedford, with a long bonnet. I used to go and help Dick and he gradually let me drive it more and more. I was about twelve years old when I started driving it, but as I had driven the Fordson tractor on the farm a lot by then, it wasn't as silly as it would be today, and of course there was very little traffic about then.

One night I was driving it back across the moor having been to collect a dead cow and some very smelly sheep. Dick was beside me and we had taken two men to help load as we didn't have a winch. I got back to Betor Cross where I was stopped by a roadblock. I thought that the police would nail me

35

for driving so I pulled my cap down over my eyes and didn't get out. They were looking for some dangerous prisoners that had escaped from Dartmoor Prison. There were some armed soldiers there and the young officer, who was a bit keen, decided to look in the back of the lorry which was sheeted down. He undid the sheet and my two helpers, who were in the back as there wasn't room in the cab, popped their heads over the side. They frightened the life out of the officer who probably thought for a moment that he'd found the prisoners. There was some confusion and then I drove off a bit quick.

One day we were sent by Father, who didn't know about my driving, to look for some hounds that we had lost around the old quarries at Drewsteignton. When we got there we saw three dead hounds floating in the water, but they were right over the other side and there was no way we could reach them. So Dick stripped off, swam out and dragged them in. He told me that he hadn't swum since he was a small boy, and he was getting on by then. I couldn't swim at all and I was very frightened that he would drown as well as the hounds.

We were bringing back a dead cow in the old lorry one day and when we turned the corner in Chagford Square the cow rolled over, smashing through the rotten sideboard and landing on the pavement right outside Lloyds Bank. That caused a bit of excitement while we struggled to get the cow back in and rope her down.

Bunchy and I were sent out on the tractor into the middle of the moor, far from any road, to collect a cow that had died. It was halfway down a very steep hill. We couldn't take the tractor down there, so we ran a rope down and tied it to the cow. Bunchy got on the tractor and opened her up. The tractor wheels started to spin so he tried jumping up and down on the seat to make it grip. Unfortunately, the spring that supported the seat broke. He fell over the back of the tractor and rolled down the hill towards me. I just collapsed in laughter. Luckily the tractor stalled or we would have been chasing a wild tractor across the moor.

Mother and I were collecting a carcase using the tractor with the horse trailer. There was only the old farmer to help, so we unhooked the tractor, blocked the trailer wheels, ran a rope through the trailer and then pulled the carcase into the trailer. We used this method often, but on this occasion, just as we had almost got loaded, the trailer ran over the blocks and rolled off down a very steep hill with the old farmer inside. He was shouting, "Whoa you bugger! Whoa!" Once again I couldn't stop laughing.

Father was driving the early Standard Fordson pulling an old four-wheeled horsebox trailer with a dead cow in the back. We were going down Betor Hill when the hitch pin broke. The trailer ran into the back of the tractor. I was riding on the footplate and jumped forward out of the way, but in doing so I knocked it out of gear. The brakes weren't up to much and we took off down the hill. I had never been so fast on a tractor. Luckily we didn't meet anything.

CHAPTER 2

1948-1953: Post-war farming, hunting and racing

I was so happy to leave school. I was firmly of the belief that I was really a stupid no-hoper. I was much happier now that I was back working with horses and farm animals and using my hands. All the jobs that I had helped with during school holidays I could now do all the time and I was keen to learn more.

I spent the first winter after I left school helping to re-make a huge Devon bank – nothing to do with money, but the name of the partition between our Devon fields. This particular bank had been neglected for many years. The willow trees on the top hung far out over the edges. There was meant to be a ditch on both sides but they had both long since filled with earth. We had to cut off the willow using axes (chainsaws were not around) and then dig out the ditches by hand using a long-handled Devon shovel to throw the earth onto the top of the bank, which of course got higher as we worked. As the ditches had been blocked for many years the whole area was a bog so we continually got stuck, often losing our wellies with resultant wet feet as we hopped about trying to get them back on.

Cecil Perryman, the old farm worker who was teaching us to do all this, often used to stand back from the work, light his pipe and survey our efforts. I asked him why he did this.

"Johnny," he said, "if you stand back and look at your work from a distance you can see if it looks all right." He went on to say that if you look at any situation in life from a distance, you may see the answer to problems very easily. What a wise thing for an old farm worker to say. It has served me well over the years.

Although the war had been over for three years there was still rationing. Of course we were largely self-sufficient as we had our own eggs, milk, and vegetables. And we used to keep a few pigs, so we were never short of bacon. An old butcher man used to come and slit the pig's throat. He used a fire to burn all the hairs off the pig and then butchered the carcase up for us.

Father had bought one of the first tractors in the parish in 1940. It was a brand new Standard Fordson and it had come with a Ransome two-furrow plough. That made ploughing much faster than the single furrow horse plough, but we still worked horses on the farm.

I was quite unaware that I was seeing the beginning of the biggest change in farming since Saxon times.

Our carthorse, Rosie, was helped out by Father's hunters or any of the young horses that Father bred. During the winter I used to haul dung out to the fields using Rosie to pull a tipcart and make a line of heaps of dung right across the field. We would have to go back and spread these heaps with a dung fork another day. I hauled mangles from a cave – a heap of mangles that had been covered with straw and earth to protect them from the frost. We used them to feed the cows. There was always wood to be cut off the banks and hauled home for the fire. Hay had to be cut from a rick. We used a big special knife to cut the hay out. It was much too heavy and dangerous for me to use when I was little, but now I could use it.

In the spring we used to chain harrow and roll the grass fields to get ready for hay-making. We had to work down the ploughed fields with harrows to get them ready for planting crops.

We still used to do most of this work with horses as fuel for the tractor was still in short supply. Perhaps Father didn't like paying for it. We and the horses were practically free.

Mother loved to ride thoroughbred horses. She bought a thoroughbred horse that was called Merry that I imagine was cheap as he was in a very poor condition and developed strangles. This nearly killed him, but Mother managed to get hold of some of the new wonder drug called penicillin. How she managed this I will never know, as I believe it was only available in army hospitals at the time. It worked wonders with him. He went on to win several races, but Mother was getting short of money and couldn't refuse a very good offer for him. He later dead-heated the Foxhunters' Chase at Cheltenham. I loved riding him, but never got to ride him in a race.

We had a lot of snow that winter. A fallen tree blocked the lane that went to Gidleigh. Mother and I used to gallop up the lane and jump the tree trunk. This was how I learned how to jump. It was a great buzz.

We were living at Woodlands at Murchington for a while. I think it was for Mother's health, but Father still owned Stiniel and we eventually moved back there.

Once the war had ended, Tom Bunch, who had left to hunt the South Berks hunt during the war, came back to help Father. I was so glad to have his help and advice. He really was more like a father to me. He always called me Master Johnny. He taught me so much and we had a lot of fun together.

We were hunting one day near Crockernwell. There was a trappy bank that had a thorn tree on top of the only place that we could jump over. We jumped it three times that day. My pony jinked around this thorn tree each time. And each time I got it wrong and fell into the thorns. It was very prickly and painful, but I got no sympathy from Tom who laughed and laughed at me.

One of my jobs was to take the horses to be shod in the forge at Chagford, where Arthur Palmer was the farrier. He had won a lot of shoeing competitions and was highly qualified. As I had to wait while he did the shoeing, I began asking him questions.

He said, "Well don't just stand there talking, give me a hand!"

I was totally surprised at this, but first he showed me how to take a shoe off. Then he taught me to make a shoe from a straight bar of iron. Gradually I learned how to shoe a horse. This was in the days before registration was introduced. I slowly became more proficient. In hindsight, perhaps I should have become a full-time farrier. Many years later I did register as a farrier in order to shoe my own horses.

There was a fringe benefit to learning to shoe as I was able to get the horses shod quicker so that I had time to meet my secret love. She was the very beautiful daughter of a farm labourer. I was more than a bit worried about this friendship, as she would very definitely not have been suitable in my parents' eyes. Class difference was so very great in those days. She was not only beautiful, but so nice. Oddly enough, we never got found out. Her father eventually moved to another farm near Broadclyst, so we lost touch with each other. However, I never forgot her. I met her again, more than fifty years later. I must admit that I didn't recognise her. The long black hair had become short and grey. But it was nice to see her and talk after all the years. I was much too young to think of settling down at the time that we were seeing each other.

I had my fifteenth birthday, so I was allowed to wear the pink coat at last. This is the hunting equivalent of the Marines' Green Beret. I got to wear it first at a Boxing Day meet in Chagford. I was now a real man – with a secret girlfriend as well. It was snowing and the ground was frozen hard. Father didn't want to hunt, as it was too hard for the hounds' feet and dangerous for the horses, never mind us. But he wanted to give the large crowd of spectators a good show. There is a big hill called Meldon that overshadows Chagford and he planned to gallop about on it blowing his hunting horn, and then call it a day. He sent me on to the top of the hill with strict instructions to stop the hounds if by any chance they actually found a fox. My girlfriend and I galloped up to the top of Meldon. We were on our own, so we started to cuddle and forgot all about foxes and hounds.

To my horror the hounds suddenly streamed straight past us hunting a fox. Neither of us had seen the fox go by. We couldn't get back on our horses in time to stop the hounds. The scent was very strong. The fox must have been what we called a travelling fox – one that had been visiting a vixen. Tom caught up with us and shouted that the fox wasn't the only one visiting!

That fox gave us a tremendous hunt across Dartmoor to Wistman's Wood. The going was very slippery with the horses slipping and sliding everywhere. He went to ground in an earth, reaching safety. Father refused to use the terriers to bolt him. He believed in giving best in a case like this. He told me that it was wiser to leave a good strong fox, as he would breed better foxes.

We were riding on to a meet one day and as we passed a local farm, Father stopped to greet the farmer. A small chicken jumped off the wall. A hound that was trotting along with his mouth open just swallowed the chicken whole in one gulp! Tom said, "Not a word, Master Johnny." We got away with that one.

Rapid changes were taking place in farming.

A contractor provided a portable baler to bale both hay and straw from the ricks. He used to turn up to do the threshing using a big single-cylinder Field Marshall tractor. It was the first diesel tractor that we had seen and was started with an explosive cartridge.

All the local farmers came to help with the threshing. In turn we also went to help them. Within a year or two pick-up balers were in use.

Father had a brand new Lister start-o-matic lighting plant installed. So we had electricity installed in the house and farm buildings. "Us was going all modern". We started to milk the cows with a milking machine.

Father bought an ex-army, 30-cwt, four-wheel-drive Humber truck. We used it to pull the horse trailer, do the knackering and also as a tractor on the farm. We must have been the first farm for miles around to have a four-wheel-drive tractor.

I passed my driving test on this big truck in Newton Abbot. I was really chuffed to be able to tear up my L-plates and be legal for a change.

Soon after I passed my driving test I was proudly driving our new Fordson Major EN27 down New Street in Chagford. It was a very high tractor and I felt like a king. All of a sudden the engine gave an almighty roar and away I went full-bore through the middle of the village. I tried to get her out of gear, but the lever was jammed solid and I couldn't get it to move. I was weaving in and out of the traffic, desperately trying to avoid hitting anything. People were jumping out of my way like fleas! Then I suddenly remembered that there was a lever that switched off the electrics; I desperately pushed it over and came to a halt. I was very shaken, but luckily no-one had been hurt. I rang up Father who came down to rescue me. It turned out that a rod had come off the throttle levers, leaving it wide open. It's a good thing this was forty years ago, when Chagford was a quiet country village. Today it would have been total carnage. My guardian angel must have been awake that day. I feel quite sorry for her because she has had a full-time job looking after me over the years.

Point-to-point racing was just getting started after the war and I helped Father to build a new course at West Nymph. We had to dig holes in the banks to make the fly fences. All done with pick and shovel – no JCBs around then.

Point-to-points in those days were far removed from today. Jockeys were for the most part truly amateur gentlemen riders, service officers such as Colonel Spencer and Major Ingall. They wore pink hunting coats. The horses had for the most part done a season's proper hunting. Most of the hunts used only their own course which would have river crossings, go through farmyards, cross roads and go up and down some very steep hills which might well have jumps at the top and/or bottom or even, as at South Pool, one halfway down the hill. Runners were few and the season was much shorter. Horses very seldom ran at meetings far from home.

Mother and Father ran some horses in that first year, but I was too young to ride them. I used to lead them up before the races in the paddock. I felt very important.

One day at the South Devon, I left a horse tied to the side of the lorry while I lead up another one. When I got back to the lorry the horse had disappeared. Panic set in, but I found her in a farm dairy where she had managed to upset all the pans of milk being used to make cream. From the amount of milk on her nose she'd had a good drink. I wiped her nose off, lead her back and made it to the paddock just in time. She started favourite, but soon tailed off. Father had the vet to her the next day but – surprise, surprise – he couldn't find anything wrong with her.

In those days there would be a pony race in the point-to-points. We raced over the same course and distance as the big horses. Although our ponies were smaller, they carried less weight and often our times were quicker. At last I was able to have my first ride in a race. I rode my own pony called Little Friar. This was the only ride that I had that year. It was at the Eggesford course at Willey Farm near Sticklepath. This was a very hilly course that twisted all over the place. It even had a water-splash at the bottom of a very steep hill.

I was taken to the White City in London where I saw Harry Llewellyn win the King George V showjumping competition. I was so fired up watching this that I decided that I wanted to become a showjumper. My parents agreed that I should do a showjumping course at Porlock Vale riding school with the late Tony Collings who had won the first Badminton event on a horse called Remus. This was a great experience as he had some of the best horsemen in the country there as instructors, including Major Hern.

On that course I fell very heavily for a really lovely, classy girl of noble birth. I was still very young and I don't think that she knew that I existed. She later became one of our leading lady show-jumpers. I never met her again. Such is life.

Back home after the course I rode a horse at Minehead called Ruddy Pip. Mother had bought him to go racing. It was a high-class race and the favourite was one of the best horses in the country. We came to the last fence together. My horse hit it very hard and I fell off. I broke some ribs that proved to be very painful.

I rode Ruddy Pip at the Dartmoor, at Thynacombe near South Brent. It was a very fast race. The bottom corner of this course had the camber all the wrong way. I knew he was clever on his feet so I cut this corner very tight. This got me out in front, but Pip did his trick of hitting a fence hard. This time I didn't fall off, but my thumb went through the ring on the top of the old-fashioned hunting breastplate. I couldn't get it out, so I had to jump all the drop fences sitting very far forward like a flat race jockey. We won, but I had broken my thumb!

I had a couple of rides later in the season and managed to stay on board. I was 'also ran' on both of them, but all the time I was getting more experience.

The next year I went with Mother to buy a horse called Dundee that was being sold by the Admiral in charge of the Britannia Naval College at Dartmouth. I tried him out over some steeplechase training fences and he proved to be a terrific jumper. We were invited to have lunch with the Admiral which turned out to be a very grand affair. There were lots of knives and forks. I had to keep peering around the large bunch of flowers in the middle of the table watching Mother carefully in order not to let the side down.

I rode Dundee in several races over the following year. He was the most exciting jumper that I ever rode, but he only really stayed for two miles and all the races were run over three.

I rode him at Dunnabridge, a moorland course that was very rough going by modern standards, but I loved it. We even had to jump a small river and cross the main road. Mother had won several races over this course before the war. In her day all the fences were stone walls.

I don't know why, but Dundee started favourite. I was jumped off him at the first fence. As I lay on the ground another horse and jockey were spinning in circles on the landing side of the fence. Every time I tried to get to my feet he ran me over again. It turned out that he had broken a rein so he could only turn circles. He gave me a real knocking about!

There were no cattle grids or gates on the moor then, so Dundee galloped several miles home to Stiniel.

He later had tendon trouble. Mother managed to get him X-rayed in the people hospital at Exeter. He was the first horse I saw X-rayed. The nurses made a lot of fuss over him, bringing him all sorts of titbits. His tendon was badly damaged, but after a long rest he was able to go hunting for several more seasons.

Dundee never did win a race.

The next year was the most successful season that I was ever to have. I bought a small mare called Snowsock. She had jumped around Cheltenham before I bought her, but was still a maiden. She was the safest jumper that I ever rode and she stayed forever, but wasn't very fast. This meant that I had to use her all the way. I won my first race on her at Willey. In hindsight this was the ideal course for her.

I next rode her at South Pool. This course had a very long steep hill that had a fence halfway down it and you just felt you were flying when you jumped it. We were well beaten coming into the last fence. Three horses that were in front of me fell all in a heap. I could see no way out of the mess, but Snowsock picked her way through so cleverly. Billy Williams, who was having his first ever ride, was on the outside of us and went on to win. I was second. Billy became a well-known professional jockey. His son is now a racehorse trainer.

I went up to the Tiverton Staghounds races where I had a spare ride on a little cob for a local farmer. The farmer told me that Ivan Knott, who was a senior jockey at the time, had schooled this cob over a sheet of galvanised iron the week before. What he didn't tell me was that the cob had turned upside down. Ivan had suggested that I should take the ride on this cob as he knew that I would ride almost anything.

I was told to just hunt the cob around. I didn't think that I had a hope in hell of winning. I was thrilled to bits, and so was the farmer, when I managed to finish third.

I was given another spare ride that day on a horse called Timosity. I was in the jockey's tent changing to ride him when a jockey came into the tent laughing his head off. We asked him what the matter was.

"There's a horse out there that is being led round by two men using bull poles. He's got a muzzle on as well."

To my horror I found out that this horse was to be my ride. The owner told me that on no account was I to put my feet forward as this horse would try to bite them – and I was also told that he would turn savage if I hit him. To make matters worse he was a really ugly brute who didn't look like he would be able to gallop on. I managed to get a good start, landing first over the first fence. Every time anybody tried to pass him Timosity opened his mouth wide and had a go at them. I managed to keep in front all the way. We hit the last fence very hard, but still managed to scramble home in first place.

I rode Snowsock in another race and I think I finished second on her.

Looking back on it, this must have been my most successful day's racing ever.

I rode Timosity again at Dunnabridge and managed to win again. I was told that we were 100 to1 with the bookmakers. I didn't bet and as I rode as an amateur I never had a shilling from the owner.

I was taking a very smart farmer's daughter to a pub that evening when a well-known local bookmaker came up to me. He wasn't being very nice. He called me some rather nasty names. He then told me that some men had put bets on my horse at the last minute and all at the same time. Of course they had managed to collect a tremendous amount of money.

I had saved several weeks' wages to take the girl out. Father was only paying me about two pounds a week for farm work. I certainly had never been paid for the ride by anybody, so I was taking the flak for nothing.

I am told that girl is now worth a million pounds!

I rode Timosity once more, but he was completely outclassed and finished well down the field. I got a tremendous bollocking from the owner, so I told him what to do with his horse.

A different jockey rode him for the next race. Unfortunately, the horse had a very bad fall and the jockey was killed. I never heard what happened to the horse after that.

My guardian angel must have been looking out for me again.

I was offered a spare ride on a pony called Egmont Gorse. This was a real step up the ladder as his owner, a Mr Nightingale, trained some really good horses. I rode him at the Lamerton races. Frank Ryall, who was the very top jockey around, rode Lonesome Boy in this race and they were hot favourites. The going was very heavy, which suited my pony as he was strongly built. After a real ding-dong of a race, I managed to win. I was on cloud nine!

Years later in the 1980s I had a very spooky experience at the Lamerton course. My daughter Honor had a ride there. I had only just come out of hospital after a heart attack and I was in a bad way. I was standing beside the last fence for her race and as the horses passed us an old man dressed in a 1930s style of clothing said out loud, "I remember a lady called Arden winning a race here in the 1930s. She was pregnant at the time."

My Mother did win at Lamerton and I was the passenger, but as I wasn't born until the end of December it couldn't have been that obvious that she was pregnant. In those days I'm sure Mother wouldn't have told anybody; it just wasn't the done thing. When all the horses had passed I looked around for him. There were only a few people by the last fence and the old man was nowhere to be seen.

Was he some kind of ghost? I shall never know.

If only the rest of my racing career had been as successful as that season which included my wins on Timosity and Egmont Gorse. My hopes were very high for the next year. However, Lady Luck deserted me with a vengeance. I had lots of good rides booked. All looked set for a wonderful time. But it was not to be.

I had a ride at the first meeting of the season and I was unlucky enough to have the worst fall of my life. I have no recollection of what happened.

When I came to I was in Newton Abbot hospital. I had broken both jaws and badly damaged the right hand side of my face. I was very lucky not to have been killed or brain damaged.

I was taken by ambulance to Frenchay Hospital in Bristol. I was conscious most of the time and aware that we went through Taunton, Highbridge and Bridgwater with the bells ringing and a police escort clearing the way. Mother followed us in her Talbot. She told me that she had never been through these towns so fast. Of course this was long before motorways or helicopters. The doctors operated on me straightaway, but I had to spend almost the whole of the season in hospital.

I had both my jaws wired together. I lived on soup that I had to suck between my teeth.

I did however manage to make friends with a German night nurse who taught me a little bit! She was so lovely!

When I got home I rode some gallops with my jaws still wired up, but I couldn't race again that year.

I had to go back to Bristol to have the wire removed and on the way back from Frenchay I said to Mother that I fancied some fish and chips as my first solid food for months. We stopped in Cullompton to buy some. I walked over to the shop and tripped over the little gutter at the side of the street. Poor Mother rushed over to pick me up. She was so worried that I might have damaged my face. As luck would have it all was well, but when I tried to eat the fish and chips my tongue kept getting in the way.

So it was no winners that season and I remember that the girlfriend of the time went off with somebody else.

She may not have needed me – but the Nation did!

49

CHAPTER 3

1953-1955: National Service

A few weeks after the wires were removed from my jaws, my call up papers came in the post.

I had to report to Warwick.

On arrival there I made an unwise remark about how rusty the tank was that was parked by the main gate. I was given the job of trying to clean it up with a small brush. I soon learned to keep my big mouth shut.

We spent time just doing fatigues, waiting for the next draft to arrive. One day a group of us were detailed to move a concrete sentry box from one side of the road to the other. Why they wanted this done, we had no idea. We managed to tip it over and, as it was round, it took off down the hill and smashed into the officers' mess, making one hell of a mess. Funny thing – we were on our way to Lincoln that very night!

We had to change trains at Birmingham and had to change stations as well. As we made our way through a park one of the lads swung around to hear what somebody was saying. He had his tin helmet packed in the end of his kit bag, as we all did. The swinging kit bag hit a civilian on the head and knocked him out. That took a bit of sorting out.

Next morning at Lincoln we met our sergeant, Waxy Turner, whose task it was to turn us into real fighting soldiers in a few weeks before we were sent to some place called Korea. He was the best sergeant I ever met. I don't think any of us knew where Korea was, let alone anything about the hellish war we were about to be sent into.

Many of these lads had never left home before and were in tears. None of us wanted to be in the army, let alone be sent off to fight wars we knew nothing about. I had been to boarding

51

school and compared to that Army life was easy. I coped easily and became the leading recruit.

We went off to the rifle range in open trucks, but our driver got it all wrong and tipped us out into a ploughed field. Rifles and boxes of ammunition dropped out of the sky on top of us. Luckily none of us was seriously hurt.

Another time we were in the deep concrete rifle butts hoisting up the targets. A halt was called for lunch and as it was a boiling hot day we all got out in front of the targets to flop on the grass. Suddenly a machine gun opened up. The bullets were thudding into the ground and smashing into the targets. Never have a bunch of recruits moved so fast. It turned out that a corporal had been trying to help a lad take aim by lying beside him saying left a bit, right a bit. He then said, "Higher." The lad thought he'd said, "Fire!" and pulled the trigger. What a bit of luck that he missed us all.

I was still very weak from hospital, lack of exercise and not being able to eat properly. I collapsed several times on marches. Luckily for me someone checked on my background and my posting to Korea was cancelled. Instead I was sent to The Veterinary Corps at Melton Mowbray.

I became a horse transport driver, driving a pair of horses to a General Service Wagon. This was just my cup of tea, but I also had to become a war dog trainer and I was not so keen on this as we had to be very hard on the guard dogs. I was soon moved onto tracking dogs and was much happier with them. We were often called out to assist the police.

One night we went somewhere on the east coast to track a gun-carrying villain who was on the run in the sand dunes by the sea. My dog and I were accompanied by a large policeman who was carrying a rifle. It was very rare to see armed police in those days and I was more than a bit scared. The dog had picked up the scent and I suggested to the policeman that perhaps it would be wiser if he didn't carry his torch in front of his body, but held it to one side. He did as I suggested and moments later a bullet smashed it to pieces. Before he had recovered the dog and I were hiding in the sand.

Another night we were called out to find an old person who had wandered off into the night. We found him, but we were too late. He had died of exposure. Very sad.

Now I was told I was going to be posted to Kenya. I went home on embarkation leave. On my last day of leave I rode a young horse of Mother's called Cabin Hill in a race at Newton Abbot. We were approaching an open ditch when a nearby steam train blew its whistle. Cabin Hill shied sideways and we turned a somersault over the fence. I was conscious, but couldn't move or feel my legs. I had to stop the St John's ambulance men from dragging me to my feet. In those days if you could stand you were better. I spent several days in Newton Abbot hospital waiting to be moved to Stoke Mandeville. It was a frightening experience, but, as luck had it, the feeling came back and I was discharged.

I had missed the boat to Kenya. The poor lad who went in my place was killed by the Mau Mau.

Count Robert Orrsich who was one of the founders of the Royal Windsor Horse Show and the very top hack showman of the day, came to the remount depot to give us a lecture on breaking wild horses.

The Army had a horse that had bucked all of us off. We used to take bets to see who could stay on longest. So of course the Count was presented with this horse. We didn't believe that he would be able to ride it as none of us cocky young lads could cope. We made sure the horse was well stoked with oats. The Count lunged the horse in the school. The horse put on a terrific show. We all watched with baited breath. Was he going to get on? He stopped the horse. A corporal who was a qualified army roughrider was assisting him. They put hobbles on his front legs and a ring on the girth and rigged ropes in a sort of W running from the Count's hand through the ring and on to the hobbles. He had the horse on the lunge and every time the horse bucked he pulled the rope which brought the horse down on his knees. After he had done this a few times, the Count told the corporal to get on. The procedure was done a few more times. The horse never bucked again while I was there.

We were always short of help. There was a large oval track and we used to turn out a lot of horses at a time. One of us would ride behind them so we could exercise any number of horses all at once. In the meantime the rest of us would do the mucking out.

Night guard in the remount depot was quite a frightening experience. It was badly lit and in a poor state of repair. Doors and windows would bang and creak in the wind. You were on your own, unarmed, and this at a time when the I.R.A. was raiding army depots in Britain. Away down in Melton you could hear the noise of the steam trains shunting etc. My God, it felt a very cold place to be.

One night I was on Main Gate guard. It was two o'clock in the morning and snowing hard. A car arrived at the barrier and the driver started blowing his horn. I dropped the blanket I had over my shoulders and walked over carrying my rifle as I would have carried my shotgun at home. Thinking it was a civilian car bringing some late-night revellers back, I told the driver not to make such a noise. Just my luck it was the officer in charge of the Midland Brigade who had been stuck in the snow and sought refuge at our camp. My feet didn't touch the ground for some time.

Another night I was on line guard in the War Dog School. I had my guard dog, Hector, with me. He was a top Army Demonstration dog who had taken part in displays all over the country. I had complete faith in him. We were allowed to take a short break during the night as we were the only ones on guard all night. I sat down in the guardroom and fell asleep, confident that nobody could possibly get past Hector. I woke with a start to find it was broad daylight. I looked at the guard book. It was signed by the orderly officer with the comment, 'Both guard and dog sound asleep. See you in the office at nine o'clock.'

I was completely baffled as to why Hector had let me down. So there I was on defaulter's parade with all the usual nonsense.

"Hat off! Belt off! Quick march!" bawled the corporal. The officer asked what I had to say.

"Guilty," I replied, but I was permitted to ask the orderly officer how he had got past Hector.

"Oh, very simple," he said. "I was his first trainer."

*

54

Rumours began to circulate that we might be involved in The Coronation.

Never volunteer for anything was the wise saying, but someone seemed to have volunteered us.

One day we had to collect a large number of horses from Melton station. They had come from Germany, had brands of all sorts and many were in rather poor condition. They were all old horses that had served with the German and Russian armies during the war.

The army selected those of us who could already ride as they didn't have time to teach those who couldn't. We were issued with brand new officer's saddles which had been in some army store. These saddles and bridles were very dry and needed lots of work to make them supple. The bits and stirrups were all made of burnished steel that went rusty if you so much as looked at it. We had to clean it with a mixture of Brasso and sand put on a rag and wrapped around the steel. When we were satisfied that we had got it clean we then burnished it by rubbing with a burnishing pad. This was a piece of leather with what looked like chain mail fixed to it. On no account could you let your hands touch the steel, or it would mark. Any moisture would turn all the steel back to rust. Almost all old saddles and harness were fitted with it. I believe the Army still uses it.

A large number of our lads had only ridden in racing stables. They all rode with short leathers, much to the disgust of the army-trained N.C.O.s. After trying for sometime to alter their style, the Army gave up trying. We were very shorthanded and there just wasn't time.

While still at Melton we went out on road exercise. Some of the lads thought their horses were better than the others. Somebody had the idea of a race across country back to the depot. We were off like the clappers. We ignored the shouts of the lance corporal. I don't remember who won, but I do remember the unholy row afterwards, not helped by the arrival of an extremely angry farmer. We were all confined to barracks.

Soon after this we loaded our horses onto a steam train. The railways used to move a lot of horses in those days, using either cattle wagons or special horseboxes that had a compartment for the grooms with a hatch so that we could check on the horses.

I can't remember which station we came into in London, but we had a purpose-built temporary camp situated in Hyde Park between the Cavalry barracks and the Serpentine. It had a high wire security fence and duckboards down to make pathways. We slept in tents that took four of us at a time. The horses were stabled in the type of portable loose boxes we still see at shows, and watered at long troughs. There was a detachment of Air Force men who looked after the Air Force Officers' horses that were also in the camp.

There were some Canadian Mounties there as well.

It was early spring and a lovely time to be in Hyde Park. We ate our meals in the Cavalry barracks. The food we had there far surpassed the awful efforts of our own cooks at Melton.

So we had smart blue walking-out uniforms, good food, horses and lots of girls around. This was proving to be a better Army.

An alley was created covered with flags and bunting. Loudspeakers blared, soldiers shouted and waved football rattles. We rode the horses through it over and over again until they took no notice. We had some hairy moments at the beginning, but they all got used to it.

We rode these horses right through the middle of London in the early morning, using blankets instead of saddles to save our highly-polished ones.

A Major Redgrave was in charge of us. He was a Household Cavalry officer and more than a bit upmarket. He came on parade riding a black charger that promptly started to really buck. We lads thought he didn't stand a chance, but to our amazement he got the better of his horse. He had, of course, gone up miles in our judgement. He was a kind and thoughtful officer to us lads. On several occasions he gave me and another lad, who was a professional jockey, leave so that we could take racing rides. I still only rode as an amateur.

The racing bug was a weakness we all had. One day we were exercising the horses on Rotten Row when the betting started as to who had the fastest horse. Off we went, but as we followed the bend around in front of the barracks we galloped full tilt into a troop of cavalry in all their ceremonial uniform.

We caused a major upset. Several of them fell off. We shot back into our stables and quickly swopped our horses with the Mounties so there were no sweating horses around our stables. Of course they knew whose horses had been involved, but they didn't know who the riders were.

We thought we were really in trouble right up to our necks, but oddly enough nothing more was ever heard about it. Perhaps the good Major helped us out?

My future wife, Sally Yandle, and her sister provided the horses for a cowboy show in London at this time. The cowboy was very good with the rope, but not so keen on riding the buck-jumping horse she provided. I became the cowboy rodeo rider. This mare really would buck-jump with her head between her knees. I had to start her by brushing her quarters with my stetson. She would really play the game, but when I felt it was time to stop I would pull her head up and yell, "Whoa!", but to the delight of the crowd she managed to drop me sometimes.

One day I spotted Sally's lorry parked on the edge of Hyde Park. I was wearing my blue walking out uniform. There was nobody about so I climbed into the cab to wait for her to come back. Two sheepish-looking girls, one of them Sally, came out from behind some bushes where they had been hiding. They had thought I was a policeman and were hoping that I would go away.

Horses would be ridden by senior officers including Field Marshals and Generals. As they often came to ride out, all saluting was stopped as we couldn't go two yards without saluting – and saluting could be tricky when carrying saddles or haynets.

Most, if not all, of these officers had been in the army before the war when they would have had to learn to ride.

The great day arrived. We rode the horses to Wellington Barracks where we got our riders mounted. We met them outside Westminster Abbey. Of course, it had to rain and we had to use our groundsheets to keep our precious polished saddles dry. When we had sent them off on the parade, we were marched off behind them. Lo and behold, we found ourselves swept into the procession. There were grandstands lining the route and there was no escape. With haynets, brooms, shovels and grooming kit, people must have wondered who on earth we were. Some bright person eventually managed to get us out of the procession.

Suddenly, it was all over. We loaded the horses onto the train. Major Redgrave and his wife came to see us off. We all spontaneously cheered them – the only time I saw that happen in the army.

Melton was an awful anti-climax after all that. It was back to reality with a bump, but we were soon back on the train again, this time heading for Edinburgh. We had a much smaller number of horses. They were all greys for the Scots Greys to ride as escorts to the Queen during her Coronation procession in Scotland.

It was after dark when we arrived at the stables. The lights didn't work, so we did the best we could to make our horses comfortable without lights. When we got into our barracks we found we were covered in black paint. Some really bright spark had had the stables painted, but not left time for them to dry.

The state of the horses had to be seen to be believed. A really desperate morning followed as we tried everything to clean them up.

Edinburgh was not a patch on our time in London. However, we didn't stay there nearly as long. I went with another lad to see The Royal Highland Show at Alloa. The thing that surprised us during the train journey was the number of horses still working on the farms we passed. By then it was already becoming rare to see horses on farms in England.

We had one little adventure. One night a staff car driver offered us a lift down into Edinburgh. This was a great idea – us riding in a general's car. The downside was that when we came to go back to barracks we couldn't find the car. We thought it had been stolen and had a nasty time until we eventually found it, not parked where we thought we'd left it.

Thinking about it now, I realise that during that trip to Edinburgh I rode on a tram for the last time.

The Argyle and Sutherland Highlanders were stationed at the same barracks. The Argyles didn't take much notice of us: not so with The Household Cavalry. They had some really nasty fights. We kept our heads down and stayed very quiet.

The Argyles used to enjoy sword-dancing. This looked more than a bit dangerous to me, so I didn't try it.

Parades over, it was time to go back to Melton on the train with our horses. It proved nothing short of a nightmare. We were shunted into every siding between Edinburgh and Melton. Supplies of food and water had to be bought or scrounged by us. It was as if the Army had simply forgotten us. In fact Pompey, the drum horse, died on this nightmare trip. If it had happened in this day and age there would have been public outrage.

Most of these old horses were put down after the Coronation. We just had to keep our mouths shut and do as we were told.

*

I had become very friendly with a beautiful girl who was a Rank starlet (a seven-pound-claiming film star!). She was not only beautiful, she was kind and generous, which was a great help as Army pay was only about a pound a week. She also brought along some of her mates on blind dates. It made me very popular with the lads.

We kept the friendship going for some time. The next winter I stayed with her in London for a weekend. I didn't have a pass from the army, so I was taking a chance. Of course I stayed too long (I wonder why?) and I missed the last train back to camp. I was standing on the platform wondering what to do when a friendly porter said that he could get me a ride back to Leicester in the guard's van of a goods train. When I got to Leicester, I still had the best part of twenty miles back to camp. It was in the early hours of the morning. I didn't have any money left, so a taxi was out of the question. I set off to walk, hoping for a lift. It started to snow hard. I walked nearly all the way. I was running out of time to get back before reveille. I knew I would be missed then and in more trouble. At the last moment, a van driver picked me up just outside Melton. I told him what trouble I was about to get into and he dropped me outside the camp gates. I made it by the skin of my teeth.

Oh, by the way, the starlet did make it big for a time.

When I was next home on leave I went to a party with Sally that went on all night. Father and I still didn't get on. I got home just as he was getting up. I staggered up the back stairs as he came down the front stairs. He soon started shouting for me to help him on the farm. I got changed, had a cup of tea and set off to work. In the afternoon he sent me to harrow a ploughed field. The sun was hot. My head was suffering and I fell asleep as the Standard Fordson chugged across the field. I was rudely awoken by the tractor running slap into the bank around the field. The engine stalled – and that tractor had to be started by swinging the starting handle which was firmly buried in the earth bank. I had to walk back to the farm to collect a pick and shovel to dig the starting handle free. As luck would have it, I managed to restart and get going just before Father came up to see how I was getting on. Luckily he didn't notice how crooked some of the work I had done was.

Soon after this I was allowed to go home on compassionate grounds as poor Mother was again very ill. My National Service ended while I was on leave and she died shortly afterwards.

CHAPTER 4

1954-1962: Marriage; family; hunting; livery; and early horse-driving adventures

My world started to fall apart after Mother died. Father and I had never got on. Mother had been the peacemaker. I couldn't cope with his drink problem and his rages. I felt that there was no point in trying to make things work. I had to leave the farm.

Mr and Mrs Les Kennard offered me a job helping them train their racehorses. They had a farm at Sheldon near Honiton. They had started training professionally after having trained point-to-point horses successfully for a number of years near Plymouth. My girlfriend, Sally, had worked for them when they first started. As she was now living with her mother in Honiton, this suited me well.

I spent a happy summer helping the Kennards with the farm and horses. They were very kind to me. Les asked me to go up to Sussex to collect a large horse box from near Brighton. Another lad had a motorbike, so we went off to fetch this huge lorry home. It was the biggest lorry I had ever driven, but we made it safely back.

I was getting a few point-to-point rides, but without Mother's horses and back up, and having missed three seasons from accident and army service, I had to start pretty much from scratch again and I wasn't getting any really good rides.

I was getting very despondent at my lack of success. I did, however, manage one winner at the East Devon races. Oddly this was on a horse called by the strange name of Black Forty-Seven that I had bought at Ascot a few years earlier, but had then sold on. Little did I realise that this was to be my last ever winner.

My sister, Tacker, wanted a gypsy caravan moved from near Bristol back to Devon. I was going to take a Landrover and

61

trailer to do the job, but it was suggested that we drove it back with a horse. A local farmer who still used horses lent me one and a racehorse trainer agreed to take it to Bristol as he was going that way. Sally said she'd come as well, although in those days the idea of us two young ones away in a caravan on our own was very naughty! Kips, my lurcher also came.

We spent a lovely leisurely summer working our way back to Devon. Of course, there weren't any motorways in those days, and there was much less traffic on the roads. The weather was good, and we found plenty of work on farms that we passed. We spent several weeks picking strawberries at Cheddar.

I bought one of the first Lambretta scooters to come into the country. This was a great way to get about. Sally and I used it for trips to the seaside at Lyme Regis. It proved to be a long hot summer, so the beach was the place to be. Our romance really blossomed during this lovely summer of 1955 and we married at Farway, near Honiton, but we couldn't afford to buy a house, nor could we find one to rent near Sheldon.

As luck would have it, I saw an advertisement in *Horse and Hound* for stables to rent at Somerford Keynes, outside Cirencester. We could just about afford the deposit, so we rode the Lambretta up there to have a look. It was by far the longest journey that we had ever undertaken on the scooter.

When we arrived at the stables we realised why the rent was so low. We had a job to push open the huge double doors that were framed by an arched building. The doors creaked slowly open to reveal an oblong stable yard that was waist high in brambles and weeds. The stable doors were hanging drunkenly open. Most of the windows were cracked or broken. It didn't look like that it had been used for years and years. I must say that our hearts sank at first. We had planned to set up a hunter livery stable, but how on earth were we going to live here and get the stables back working in time for the coming hunting season?

There was some living accommodation to the left-hand side of the arch. There were two rooms downstairs and the same upstairs. There was no bathroom, but it did have electricity.

There were coach houses at the end of the yard and a loft

and forge on the right. It came with a couple of paddocks. I later learned that the stables had been built by a Mr Macmillan for his private use, but he was killed while out hunting before the war. So the stables had remained shut up until we came along, which explained their derelict state.

I had realised by this time that I was going to be too heavy to be a professional jockey. I did, however, have hopes of becoming a racehorse trainer. This was long before motorways had even been thought of, so the move upcountry seemed wise. To try and get established as a trainer I hoped to start with the hunter liveries and to progress to doing some point-to-pointing with a horse of our own. Even if we failed to get any liveries, it would give us a house to live in and a brand new start away from home.

We were young and naïve and we hadn't a clue about running a business. But we knew that we were both capable with horses. We were full of confidence, enthusiastic and thought that we could conquer any difficulties. We moved in, put in a bathroom and set about sorting the place out.

Roy Stuart, a cattle haulier who had competed against us while we were doing gymkhanas, offered to take our horses and us up there. At that time he had only one small cattle lorry. Later he became the owner of a fleet of double-decker cattle lorries.

We had paid the rent, but that left us with very little capital, so I had to find some casual farm work to make ends meet. We advertised for some hunter liveries and got a good response. Hard work was required to clear up the weeds and brambles. We both had to become carpenters to mend and paint the stable doors, which was the first priority. We were actually cooking over an open fire in the middle of the yard to start with, using the brambles and rotten stable doors to keep the fire going.

As we had almost no furniture we went to a furniture sale at Perrots Brook, where they were selling the pub's furniture. I think that the pub was called *The Bear*. We came home with a table, some chairs and a few other items.

As soon as we could, we bought a new Calor gas cooker.

National Service involved two years' service, but it was followed by a three-year period of being 'on reserve'. To our horror the Army called me up because of the Suez crisis. I certainly didn't think it would apply to me. I found myself back in Melton and Sally was left to cope on her own.

We had already managed to get the promise of a couple of hunters for the next season. I thought that Sally was quite capable of coping with them, but she had to do it while sorting out the run-down stables.

What a futile waste of time this Army service proved to be. All of us who had been recalled were billeted in the same wooden hut. None of us wanted to be there, so we decided to be as unhelpful as we could be, without getting into too much trouble. We were just doing menial tasks around the camp. My buddy, a professional jockey called Ken Boulton, and I were given the task of painting white lines on the car park outside the officers' mess. We decided to make a real bad job of it. Nobody inspected what we had done until the next day when the white paint had dried and was impossible to remove. We got a terrific bollocking, but there was little the Army could do.

Our plan worked. We were both soon on the train home. I heard later that some of the 'good' boys were still there for Christmas, so I reckon we did the right thing.

Sally was very glad to see me home as she was needing all the help and support that she could get.

I was told that a farmer who lived in nearby Ashton Keynes had a Ralli Car trap for sale. Sally and I rode over to see it. We managed to buy it for fifty-bob (two pounds ten shillings in old money, two pounds fifty in new). We had taken with us a very old set of harness and Sally's old pony, Sue, would go in harness, so we proudly drove the trap home. We often used this old trap as we were finding petrol very expensive. Nothing changes!

I made it my business to get to know as many horsey people as possible. I made arrangements with the Vale of the White Horse Hunt secretary so that we could hunt with their hounds. He was a kindly old gentleman called Major Arnott, who lived in the next village, Pool Keynes. He was so helpful, and recommended us to several hunt members.

The master was Earl Bathurst. This was before the Bathurst and Cricklade V.W.H. amalgamated. Some of our country was up on the Cotswold Hills where we used to jump a lot of walls. We had some very heavy clay country in the Minety and the surrounding vale country. The horses that had been hunting in the Cricklade Vale would come in covered in thick clay. It was almost impossible to get them clean. As I had been taught that it was not correct to wash them off, I was reluctant to wash. But in desperation we tried washing with warm water using lots of old towels which we could buy cheaply from a second-hand furniture dealer.

The fences were big with ditches on both sides. That meant we got a lot of jumping in, which was a nice bit of fun as we had very little jumping at home on Dartmoor.

Everybody was friendly and we kept getting more horses at livery. By the end of the season we felt that we'd made a good start.

I did, however, hate having to chase owners for money. I used to get so embarrassed at having to do this.

The next summer Sally told me that she was pregnant. This was not planned and I got the blame as it was clearly all my fault!

One night Sally woke me up to say that the baby was on its way and that I had better get the car out as quick as possible. We had borrowed a Singer pre-war sports car to be ready for this event, but nothing on God's earth would make her start that night. I tried the starter until the battery was nearly flat and then I swung the starting handle with no more luck.

Sally was shouting at me to hurry up. We didn't have a phone to ring for a taxi. Suddenly I spotted our horsebox and climbed into the cab. Thank goodness she fired up straight away, but Sally said she couldn't possibly climb into the high cab. I dropped the ramp and chucked a bale of straw in for her to sit on. She was grumbling a bit I can tell you. Off we went to The Querns Hospital in Cirencester. A nurse came out when we arrived, looking more than a bit puzzled by our arrival in the lorry. I quickly dropped the ramp and the sight of Sally explained all.

Our son, Stephen, arrived very quickly afterwards. He was born in this lovely hospital where the foxes would come out to play on the lawns. The foxhound kennels were just across the road.

It was the 17th May 1957 and I was back in Sally's good books.

She wasn't long out of hospital when I heard that there was a flapping race meeting to be held at Brinkworth. We decided to take Tuesday, an old racehorse that I owned, to try him there. It was a flat race meeting, but the course was very hilly with some very sharp turns. I rode him in the first race and won it easily.

There was a ladies' race later in the afternoon. We could both see that Tuesday was fine to race again and that Sally would have a very good chance of winning. I had told her that she really shouldn't ride as she was only just out of hospital. There was no dissuading her – but she was wearing a skirt.

I swapped my trousers for her skirt and off they went. Sally won. The trouble was that she was so weak that she couldn't stop Tuesday. I was watching from the lorry cab. I forgot all about the skirt and ran out onto the track to grab him. The crowd thought that this was the funniest thing they had ever seen.

We found out that there were two more flapping meetings coming up close to home. The next meeting was at Minety. They had a race over hurdles with an open ditch fence at the bottom of a hill. We decided to run two horses, Toss Up and Tuesday, in this race. As Tuesday had done so well at Brinkworth the bookies made us favourite. Sally rode Toss Up who had run in several pony races in point-to-points and was a nice safe jumper, but certainly no racehorse.

There were some very rough types riding in this race. I believe they came from the Bristol area. To make sure that they didn't interfere with Tuesday I got away in front. Tuesday was very fast so I was able to stay there. As we came down the hill to the open ditch two other runners came alongside me. Tuesday loved to race on the flat, but was never the best of jumpers and he took it into his head to run out. We took both of the other horses with us.

This left Sally and Toss Up to jump the fence and find themselves in front. Sally went on to win. My God, there was an unholy row about this as the other boys were certain that I had done it on purpose – which I most certainly hadn't.

The next meeting was at South Cerney. We ran Tuesday again, but I let a former flat race apprentice ride him. The same Bristol gang was there. They were determined to get revenge for the Minety race. I had warned our boy to try and keep in front of them, as I knew that Tuesday would stay the course. He was not quick enough at the start and let one of the gang get away in front. The other one had the job of trying to stop Tuesday. He managed to come up inside Tuesday on a sharp corner and forced him off the course. They both crashed into a tent that was the ladies' loo and turned upside down. They bolted a very frightened lady out of the tent!

Somebody told us that there was a lot of flapping racing in Wales. We managed to find out a bit about this so Derek Caswell (who had been an apprentice with Frenchie Nicholson) and I set off in my old Austin lorry to try our luck. We also took a well-bred pony that belonged to a local farmer. This pony had never raced, but had proved very fast when we had galloped it with Tuesday.

Neither of us had ever been to Wales before. We had been told some terrible tales about the Welsh, so we were a bit worried as to what our reception would be. We managed to find our way to Llangadock, arriving the day before the races in order to find some stabling. We went down to the course where some men were getting the field ready for the big day.

They gave us a very friendly reception. They told us about an old manor house that had disused stabling that we might be able to use. I believe it was called Glansevin. I think that the house itself was full of Polish people.

It was a lovely old yard. We stayed there for a week.

The racing was a real eye opener. They had trotting races as well as galloping races. We had never seen trotting races before, except on films from America.

Jockeys had to be able to ride at a light weight and wore colours as in proper racing. Some of these jockeys had been professional flat race jockeys in England, but had probably been banned for some misdemeanour. They were very tough men.

By riding in these flapping races I was leaving myself open to a ban on riding as an amateur in point-to-points, so Derek rode both of our horses, but I am afraid he was not experienced enough against those tough Welsh jockeys.

Tuesday finished third in his race, but the pony failed to get round the sharp corner at one end of the track and galloped straight into a river. Derek got very wet.

We were invited to a party that night. We found the Welsh most friendly.

The next meeting was at Penybont. We managed to stay at a local farm. As far as I can remember we didn't get into the money, but we still had a fun time and this time the pony got round safely.

We then went onto Llandrindod Wells races. By now we had got to know some of the other competitors. I was really excited by the trotting as I could see that my weight problem didn't matter. I was getting very keen to find out more about it. Some of the trotting owners were northern businessmen. They were friendly and helpful. We went to a great party at the Metropole hotel.

We had a great time in Wales, but we were not good enough so we didn't earn any money, which had been the object of this expedition. Still, we had an exciting time. I only wish that I had been able to repeat it.

I later tried to get into trotting racing, but I never had enough money to spare. I really regret not having been able to get involved. In hindsight, perhaps I should have somehow managed to stay at Glansevin and make a fresh start in trotting racing.

I was risking a ban under the rules of proper racing for taking part in flapping racing, so I was doing all this under a false name. I don't think that I was alone in that.

The same rule applied to horses. Tuesday's real racing name was Lime Lodge. He had good flat race form before I bought him.

*

Both Sally and I thought that it would be a good idea to have a house cow. We had read an article in *The Smallholder* that praised the Dexter, so off we went to Somerset to have a look at a herd of these tiny cows. We ended up buying two cows and a calf. Little did I realise that these cows were going to be an enormous part of my life for many years.

Sally just loved these cows, but they became more than a bit of a nuisance to me as so often I had to milk them after a hard day's work. Just a couple of cows would have been all right, but Sally wanted more. To add to our difficulties we didn't own any land of our own, so we were dependent on renting land anywhere that we could. At first we managed with some small paddocks and orchards that were disused, but as the herd grew we rented some land down the Minety road.

We used to tether the cows as the fences were in a very poor condition. One night there was a terrific thunderstorm. As the cows were tethered by chain to a steel stake in the ground, we were worried that the lightning might kill them. I jumped on my pushbike and braved the really frightening storm. As I was pedalling along the lightning struck an oak tree as I was passing it. It was as if a bomb had exploded beside me. It blasted me right off the road into a deep ditch. It put the fear of God into me. I crawled out of the ditch, collected my thoughts and went on. I managed to free the cows. I was very thankful to arrive home and change into some dry clothes.

We later managed to rent some fields near to South Cerney that belonged to the Bathurst estate. There was a river and a railway line that ran through the middle of these fields. A steam train used to come along it. The drivers never seemed to be in a hurry. We sometimes hitched a lift into Cirencester with them. I don't suppose that you could do that anywhere today. We had a portable milking bail there and sold the milk to the creamery at Latton.

The amateur rules of racing caused me a lot of problems. The main one being that to stay an amateur I was not allowed to become a huntservant or work as a groom, which were the only jobs that I had trained to do, other than farm work. Strangely enough, I could run a livery stable and keep my amateur status. If I wanted to continue to ride as an amateur, running a livery stable was the only way to go. And if I needed extra money it would have to be through farm work.

At the end of the hunting season all the hunters went home to be turned out to grass for the summer, which meant that we had to look for summer work. I was asked to help a farmer milk his herd of cows. He was using a modern, four-abreast parlour for the milking and I explained that I didn't know how to work it.

"That's all right," he said, "I'll show you how to manage if you come along in the morning."

The next morning I was there bright and early.

He showed me how to milk the first four and then disappeared into his house. I struggled on as best as I could, but I was having some problems with the machine so I went over to the house to ask him for some help. His wife came to the door to tell me that he had gone to London and wasn't expected back for several days. Unlike most farmers' wives she hadn't a clue about anything on the farm, so she was no help at all. I did persuade a local cowman to come in and give me some more instruction. The worst thing about this job was that the cheque I was paid with bounced. I never did get the money.

An old farmer came into the yard to ask me to break in a horse. Of course I agreed and we rode to his farm near The Leigh to collect the horse. It was six years old and it turned out that several people had tried to break him.

The first problem was catching him. We eventually managed to chase him into the farmyard and he shot into the carthorse stables and into a stall. At least I could now get near him using the next stall. He wouldn't let me put a halter on him. He was striking out with his front feet and trying to savage me with his teeth. He was one of the wildest horses I had ever met. I finally managed to get a rope around his neck and pull his head over towards me and with help got a halter on him. He was much too wild and dangerous to try and lead out of the stable, so I tied him up using a strong cart rope. He fought like crazy. I was worried that he was going to hurt himself. The farmer didn't seem to be worried: he said that if I didn't succeed he would have the horse put down. I stayed with the horse all night and by morning he would take food and water from my hand.

I had put a carthorse collar on to Toss Up and we tied the horse to the collar so that Sally could pull him towards home while I chased him on with a hunting crop. We made it safely back.

I tried to lunge him, but all he would do was buck like some mad bronco. I could see that this was not going to be easy money.

We took the horse to a nearby farm where there was a cattle yard that was still deep in dung from the winter. I tied some sandbags onto the saddle and turned the horse loose. Calgary Stampede had nothing on the show he put on! No wonder nobody had been able to ride him before. He bucked himself to a standstill. I rigged up ropes the way that I had seen Count Orssich do. It worked a treat. Every time he bucked I pulled his front legs away.

I got Sally to leg me up and he was off again, but I had got him very tired so I was able to stay there and ride him out. We did this for several days before I was able to ride him without having to use the cattle yard first. In a very short time I was able to ride him back to the farmer that owned him, who was delighted that I had managed to get his horse going. He wanted me to take the horse out hunting for the next season.

I took him out for his first day with the V.W.H. Cricklade. The farmer pointed out two ladies who were both on very useful sorts of horses. He told me to follow them. Hounds soon found a fox and the ladies promptly set off at full gallop jumping all the big fences. As luck would have it I had been schooling my horse over some jumps so I knew he could really jump. The trouble was he would try to buck me off on landing.

I managed to keep close enough to the ladies to give my horse a lead and I also managed to stay on when he threw some more bucks. Afterwards the farmer was over the moon. I was pretty pleased with myself as well.

I asked him who on earth were these two ladies that had given me such a terrific lead. The old boy laughed and told me that they were Anne Townsend and her mother. Anne was one of the very top show jumping girls around at that time.

I later sold this horse at Ascot sales. This was before Ascot only sold thoroughbred horses. He went on to become one of the country's leading show jumpers.

As a result of my success I got several more horses to break. The big problem was to get owners to pay enough to make it worth doing.

I bought the biggest thoroughbred horse that I had ever seen from a farmer who was sending him for slaughter as he was proving to be unrideable. He was eighteen hands high and would run away as soon as you got on him. He was completely unstoppable. He would just clamp the bit between his teeth and go. If you pointed him at a fence or gate he just crashed through it and turned over. He was terrifying.

An older and wiser man that I knew told me he had a bit that might work. He brought it over for me to try. It was a huge roller gag snaffle with big rings. The horse was unable to grip this bit between his teeth and because of the very large rings he could no longer just open his mouth on the corners as he had been doing. Several times I found that I had pulled the ordinary snaffle right through his mouth in my desperate attempts to turn him.

Once we put this bit on him I found that I could control him much better.

I hunted him the next season. I had to spend a lot of time schooling him over poles to try to get him to take a short stride as his huge stride was apt to get him into trouble. I was able to run him in some maiden races in the spring. I was getting him round with some difficulty. He didn't seem to be very fast, but he stayed forever.

I knew that the Heythrop Hunt had a four-mile race at their point-to-point. I decided to try him in this race: I could only finish last or fall. I deliberately got left at the start so that I could get a good lead. I just tried to get him jumping and settled at the back. I soon began to pass some of the other horses that didn't stay so well. I was thrilled to finish in the first six out of twenty or so runners. He was still very green indeed.

A wealthy farmer came up and offered me a huge sum of money in cash. There was no way that I could turn this offer down. There is, or was, a custom of 'luck money' in the Cotswolds at this time. I planned to give this man the bit that was the answer to this horse as his luck money. His son, who was planning to ride the horse, came up to us. So I started to tell him how to ride the horse. He was very rude to me. He told me that he didn't need any advice from some little horse coper. So I took the bit home with me. Incidentally, I still have it. I have never found another horse to fit it.

I would have loved to have been able to race this horse for another season as I had high hopes of him being successful, but as usual I needed the money. I never heard of the horse again.

I was able to buy a lovely grey hunter from my old friend Mr Stooke Hallet who was a very knowledgeable dealer back home in Devon. I bought this horse in order to sell him on.

Next season I was asked to provide a hireling hunter for an American who was over here to do the season foxhunting. He was a real gentleman. I was able to hire him the hunter for as many days as the horse could do and I boxed him all over England. The American got on so well with the horse that he paid me a premium in order that he was the only person to hunt him. What a terrific season I had.

I was out hunting one day when a man had a bad fall. He was stuck in a ditch underneath his horse. The horse was thrashing about wildly and wasn't able to get out. I seemed to be the only person who realised that the man was in real danger of drowning. I leapt off my horse and rushed over to try to help him. I got into the ditch, but he was a big heavy man and didn't seem able to help me. The horse's hooves were flailing about all over the place. I had to keep dodging them. I was managing to keep the man's head above the water, but was running out of breath myself. At last some of the field realised there was trouble and came to help. They dragged both of us out. It was rather a close call. The horse was still thrashing around and had to be dragged out as well.

I was completely wet through, but still had to ride several miles to get home.

Later, to show his gratitude, the man took Sally and me out for a very good meal at *The King's Head Hotel*.

I did a lot of hunting young green horses for other people. I really enjoyed it. It gave me great satisfaction when I later saw them going well for their owners. I liked to follow well behind the hounds so that I could get on with my job, well out of everybody's way.

One day when I was doing just this near Charlton, I jumped into a field. My horse started to swerve all over the place and I wondered what on earth could be wrong with him. Then I saw a strange animal going up the other side of the field beside a wood. It was in the shadow of the trees, but seemed quite big. My horse was snorting and pricking his ears at it. I was having a job to get close. Suddenly I realised that it was Mr Westamacott crawling along the ground. He used to ride with a wooden leg that he fitted into a leather bucket. When he had fallen he had broken this wooden leg. He had lost his horse, so he was crawling along on his arms and remaining leg.

When he saw me, he started shouting at me to help him. This unnerved my horse even more and I had to tell Mr Westamacott to sit still and stop shouting, as I couldn't get my horse anywhere near him. I eventually managed to leg him up onto my horse so that we could walk back to a farmhouse to get some more help.

He was a truly remarkable old man who was still breaking horses to ride long after most of us would have called it a day. His wife was very worried that he might be hurt doing this, so she asked me to do the backing for him. I was only too glad to do this for both of them. He was still doing all the long reining and lunging and early training.

Some years later when my father had a leg amputated, Mr Westamacott was able to offer a lot of help and advice to enable Father to ride again and to hunt his hounds with only one leg. Father continued as M.F.H., even showing hounds at the Devon County Show, riding with one leg.

Trying to make a living was a bit difficult during the summer months. I found that I could often go to Ascot sales at the end of the flat racing season and buy two- and three-year-old racehorses that hadn't been successful racing. I could see that they needed time to fill out, a lot of schooling and just hacking out to make them into useful horses. I managed to do a deal with a farmer who loved horses and was close to retirement. He kept the horses on his farm. I rode them on to make them more useful and we split the profits. One day I pulled down the ramp at Ascot and to my horror lots of chickens flew out flapping their wings. They must have gone to roost the night before in the horsebox as I had left the ramp down overnight and only shut it up before I left. I ran away and hid, making out they were nothing to do with me. We did this for several years until the farmer died. The farm was then sold, so that little earner finished.

I was also buying potential polo ponies for a professional polo player as I went around the sales. I would get them ready for him to train on for polo.

I met up with a sharp dealer who told me that he knew a farmer in the New Forest who had fields full of ponies that would be suitable for the polo game.

So I took him with me in the lorry to take a look. It turned out that they were only small New Forest ponies, not nearly big enough for my job. I was disappointed and more than a bit mad that I had gone all that way. What a complete waste of time and petrol.

I suddenly thought that I might as well take home a load of these wild ponies so that I could break them in and try to sell them. The extraordinary thing was that all these ponies went on well after I had broken them in. One of them even competed at the White City show in London.

I bought a nice grey child's pony that I thought I might make a profit on. Tamsin, a local girl who helped out around the stables, was riding him about and he was going very well. She left him tied up to a ring in the stable yard while we all went in for lunch.

A farmer who I knew was very tight-fisted knocked on the door. "How much do you want for that pony in the yard?" he asked.

Knowing how hard a man he was to deal with, I asked him for twice what I knew I could hope to get. To my utter amazement he paid me the full amount in cash. I really thought that I was losing my senses. I just couldn't believe my luck. Years later I asked why he had paid so much for this pony. He replied that when he came into the yard he had seen my son, who was still very small, climb up the pony's tail to get on to the pony.

The farmer wanted it for his grandchildren, so was prepared to pay any money for such a good-tempered pony – and he thought the pony must be all right if I allowed my boy to do this. Actually, I had no idea that Stephen was in the yard and I would have had a fit if I had seen him do it. As it turned out, the pony was a great success with the family and stayed there for the rest of his life.

I've mentioned Tamsin and this seems the right time to say more about her. She lived with her grandmother in a council house in the village. She was always coming to the stables and following Sally about. I taught her to ride and she helped out a lot with the horses and with baby-sitting Stephen. One day she came and said that she couldn't wake her grandmother. We went to the house and found that the old lady had passed away. Tamsin stayed with us while things were sorted out, but nobody ever came for her – so she just stayed.

She became one of the family and lived with us for years. She was a very attractive teenager and I had to chase away a number of unsuitable males. Eventually Tamsin moved away and got married. She phoned me recently to say that she had retired! I found that really hard to believe.

I hated having to ask customers for money. I am afraid I just used to give too much credit at first.

We had a very upmarket customer who seemed such a nice guy. He never appeared to have any money, but he and his wife lived in great style with good quality horses and posh cars. I had to go around to his large country house to try and get some money. As I knocked at the back door he ran out of the front door and disappeared. His charming wife came to the door.

She said, "Oh, what a pity! My husband has just had to go out. You have only just missed him."

I waited for a couple of days to pass then I tried again. This time I went to the front of the house and took the ignition key out of the car. I then went to the back door and rang the bell. Sure enough he rushed out to his car. I caught him and actually managed to get some money.

He came to the stables at the end of the season to tell me that he was running away with somebody else's wife. He made over his horses to me to cover what he owed, so I was all right.

He left owing a lot of money everywhere else.

Sally's mother had bought a hunter for herself, but was finding it too much for her and she asked us to buy it. I duly collected it from Exmoor. It was grey and a very well-bred sort, but it was a bit quick. It had never been raced, but when we galloped it on an old aerodrome with some horses belonging to Andy Frank this little mare proved to have a good turn of foot.

I hunted her with the V.W.H. and she proved to be a nice safe jumper, so we decided to run her in some point-to-point races. We ran her at the Cricklade in a maiden race. She gave me a terrific ride and jumped like a stag all the way. Andy Frank and I had a terrific race upsides of each other. He went on to win, but I was thrilled to bits at how well she had run.

I later ran her in the members' race at the Bathurst races. The two Crew brothers were riding in the same race once again. This little mare ran very well indeed, but she was a bit small to carry 12 stone 7 pounds over three miles.

I was managing to get a few spare rides at this time. I rode a nice safe sort for a farmer who lived on the Mendips, so I got to hunt with the Mendip Farmers' Hunt. This was great fun as there were lots of walls to jump.

Nice easy winners didn't come my way, but I got some rides around the Beaufort, Larkhill, Berkley, Cotswold, Heythrop, Cricklade, Siddington, and Avon Vale courses. Terry Biddlecombe, who went on to be champion jump jockey, was riding as an amateur at this time.

I used to take horses over to Bathurst Park very early in the morning to gallop them in the park before anybody was about. We used to cross a place where five rides all met on the side of a very steep hill just after this. There is a post and rail fence with a gate in it at the foot of the hill that was usually open, but on one particular day it was firmly shut. I was on a horse that was a very bad jumper and I knew that I hadn't a hope in hell of jumping the gate or of stopping. Somehow or other I zigzagged down the hill and ran into the rails at the bottom. Later that week an old man who worked as a gamekeeper for the estate told me in the pub that he had been up there and heard us coming, so he'd shut the gate thinking that we would want to jump it.

I knew I was coming to the end of my racing career. As much as I loved the terrific thrill of galloping and jumping big fences, I was getting older, heavier and good rides just didn't exist anymore for me. It was time to call it a day.

*

Mr Sebastian Gilbey

I kept Mr Sebastian Gilbey's hunters at livery for many years. He was a director of the famous gin firm based in London.

He almost never rode out, except to go hunting. How he managed to do this I shall never know as he was not a thin, naturally-athletic type. He would go very well, but always wanted me to be close at hand in case of misfortune. This was not so easy as I was often riding a green horse.

He had a great friend, a Mr Page, who had served at Gallipoli in the First World War. He was such a nice man. After hunting we hacked back to the trailers where there was always plenty of vodka and sandwiches.

Mr Gilbey bought a grey horse from somebody that he thought he knew well. I had to take his Jaguar car and trailer to collect this horse. When I got there the groom brought the horse out and helped me to load him. After a few days this horse refused to go out of the yard. He was proving to be nappy and dangerous as he would rear. He did this like an old hand. He had been bought and vetted as a four-year-old. Of course, I hadn't looked in his mouth when I had collected him. I had a nasty thought about his age and when I looked I was horrified to find he was at least nine years old. Had the groom given me the wrong horse or worse still would people think I had worked a swop?

I rang Mr Gilbey up and asked if his vet could come and look at the horse's teeth. The vet duly turned up and swore blind that the horse was four and that I was wrong. He was one of the top horse vets of his time; he said that I didn't know what I was talking about.

I tried hunting this horse, but he would go for a bit and then chuck it in. I jumped a fence and landed in a small paddock. He refused to jump out of it, so I went over to the gate, which led onto the road. It was padlocked. A notice on the gate said that anyone found hunting on this land would be prosecuted. I managed to pull down some rails and lead this awful horse out. I told Mr Gilbey that the horse would never be any good. He afterwards sold him to a dealer who knew all his history. I was so pleased that the dealer confirmed my ageing of this horse. I never found out the real truth of this deal.

Mr Gilbey very often had friends to stay. I used to look after them when they went hunting. One day I was looking after a man who had brought his own lovely thoroughbred horse. Both horse and man were extremely well turned out. The hounds met at Charlton. They quickly found a fox. My man galloped straight at a stiff post and rails. The horse never took off and they had an awful fall. The horse suffered some nasty cuts, as did the jockey. I picked up the pieces and we all retreated to the local pub, where we had parked his posh horsebox. I bandaged up the horse and made him as comfortable as possible. Meanwhile our man had stayed in the pub to recover: this was pre-breathalyser days.

Mr Gilbey had a horse that every now and again would buck him off. He decided to sell it at Leicester horse sales. I duly took the horse there, but he failed to reach his reserve price. A Mr Lane, who was well known in the showjumping world, said that if this horse could jump round his circular school of show jumps he would give me the asking price. As I had to go home through Stratford-upon-Avon where he lived, I agreed to take the horse there for them to try. When I arrived there I was told to ride him round what to me looked a very big course of jumps. I had done a little showjumping, but I didn't know if the horse had ever done anything other than hunt. To my relief and surprise he just flew round, never touching anything. Once around was enough. I pulled up and put my hand out for the pound notes. He was as good as his word and paid up in full.

*

Early horse-driving adventures

I have always had a great interest in driving horses, although I have no real explanation for this. Among the photographs you will find one of me aged about three, wearing harness and pulling a little cart by hand.

The art of driving had nearly been forgotten. Apart from the gypsy caravans that were nearly all still horse-drawn, there were very few people driving. Those that were, were mainly driving in the showring.

I had driven horses at home and a pair during my army service. Remember at that time there were no good books or helpful videos around. The few old men that knew anything tended not to be helpful. They seemed to like to keep any knowledge they had to themselves.

I was asked to break a cob to drive for a local farmer. I knew almost nothing about breaking to harness. We had use of a paddock that was next to the churchyard. After I had done some long reining, I put him to a cart for the first time. He took off in a series of great fly-jumps. He jumped the rather flimsy hedge straight into the churchyard. To my horror there was a burial service taking place. The pony was brought to an abrupt halt by getting the wheels jammed against two gravestones. We had to take him out of the cart while the body was being lowered into the grave. There was a rather unholy row about this I can tell you!

Despite this, the cob actually came to drive easily which encouraged me to take on breaking other ponies.

I was talking to a dealer about the trotting racing. He told me that he had a trotting pony that he wanted to get broken to drive. I jumped at the chance. I thought that if I got him going the dealer might let me race him.

After long reining him and getting him to pull a log around the field, I thought that he was ready to go into a cart. Derek was helping me. The round pen, or our present trotting track, had never been thought of at that time.

We had to put the pony to the cart on the road as we didn't have a field available. I got into the cart and Derek led him off on a long rope. The pony leapt forward in a big jump. Derek

17 Ferguson T20 with belt-driven saw. Affectionately
known as 'the little grey fergie'.
Photographed at the Royal Cornwall Show.

18 Standard Fordson & Fordson Major as bought by
my father and driven by me as a youngster.

19 Stationary baler of the type used when I was driving
hay and straw lorries.

20 Honor & Clare with Peter in the snow.

21 Just One outside Stinhall, driven to a butt-cart, 1974.

22 Ride and drive to Fingle Bridge from Chagford, 1980.

23 Beauty with a stone roller at Chagford.

24 Beauty in the new Fenlands gig, 1982.

25 With Dutch tourists at the Walla Brook.

26 Receiving my prize from Willie Carson,
Cirencester driving trials, July 1991.

27 Woolley, Bracken, Pip and Vodka (with Fiver) at Pizwell, 1990.

28 Tandem of six: Bracken, Gubbins, Woolley, Pip, Dodger & Bungle, August 1990.

29 Eight-in-hand: Gubbins & Woolley, Fingle & Pip, Dandy & Bracken, Dodger & Bungle, July 1991.

30 Maggie with Solo driven to the ralli car Christmas Day, 1991.

31 Driving Dusty to a hay rake.

32 Riding Isca using Mr Allen as packhorse to feed
ponies in the snow, February 1994.

managed to scramble onto the cart. We were airborne! This pony could really trot, but the brakes and steering were not all that they should be. We were just flying along. If we could just keep turning right we would arrive back home with any luck. The trouble was that the second right turn was a T-junction on a busy road. As we thundered down to the junction we could see two of Cullimores huge gravel lorries coming along the main road. We hadn't a hope in hell of stopping the pony. I managed to trot right between the two lorries. I did have some help from the second lorry driver who was standing on his brakes.

We shot straight across the road and the pony crashed down into a large deep ditch. Somehow we both managed to stay on the cart. The pony plunged wildly about in the ditch until he managed to jump back onto the road with the cart still attached. The pony was off again with both of us clinging onto the cart for dear life, but I was able to regain control. I never got to speak to the lorry driver to give him my thanks for reacting so quickly.

We bought an unbroken trotting pony from Mr Reid at Cerney Wick. He was a lovely bright bay colt with a lot of presence. We called him Seven Springs. He took to driving like a duck to water. I had probably only had him in shafts a couple of times when I was telling everybody in *The Bakers Arms* how fast this pony was. Somebody bet me that I couldn't drive this pony to Cirencester and collect an evening paper to prove that I had been to town, and arrive back at the pub by a certain time. Of course my big mouth got me into trouble.

Tamsin volunteered to come with me. As we left the stable yard the pony swerved sharply to the left. He managed to get the yard gate jammed between the wheel and the body of the cart. Tamsin saved the day by managing to push the pony back. Then we were off like the clappers. This pony didn't know how to gallop, but he could trot for England. We arrived at Cirencester in no time. There used to be a newspaper seller outside the cinema. I told Tamsin to jump out and buy a paper while I drove around the back of the cinema and then came back to collect her and the precious paper. I knew that I had no hope of the pony standing still while she bought the paper. She leapt back on board. We made the return trip just as fast and collected the bet.

One rather sad thing that I can remember at this time is seeing a pair of carthorses pulling a Wiltshire waggon with a large load of sacks, being driven by an old farm worker. He was coming down the Oaksey road. I think this was the last horse-drawn waggon that I can remember doing an ordinary job of work. I know that we see such turnouts at heavy horse events, but somehow that is not the same as one going about its everyday work. Once again I was seeing a great change and not realising it.

I saw a set of driving harness advertised in a furniture sale down at Wylie. This was a long way from Cirencester to go on a Lambretta, but I was young and mad keen, so off I went. It turned out to be a lovely set of pre-war English harness that was in very good order. I believe I paid some twenty pounds for it. I was in real trouble when I got home. Sally thought that I had paid much too much for it. I can still manage to get into trouble today! There was almost no harness being made in England at that time. Foreign harness hadn't made an appearance, as far as I know.

I was hauling a load of firewood to *The Bakers Arms* with a four-wheeled trolley. As we went over a step in the car park the trolley broke clean into two pieces. The back half ran out onto the road. Luckily it didn't hurt anybody, but it did make the pony pulling it leap about a bit!

I used to go to Stow-on-the-Wold Fair as often as I could. We didn't have fairs like that in Devon. This was very much a gypsy fair. Most of them were still using horse-drawn caravans and carts and trolleys of all descriptions. They often used to have fights in the roads. The police never seemed too keen to interfere. While there was an official auction of horses going on, most of the gypsies preferred to sell their horses from the side of the road with much slapping of hands and spitting.

I saw a strong type of cob pulling a heavy load of scrap iron up the hill. When he got to the top of the hill his owner, who was waiting for him to arrive, shouted, "What am I bid for this grand cob?" There were several takers, all shouting different bids. A deal was quickly done with the usual slapping of hands. I happened to know the old gypsy who had sold the horse. We all trooped off to the pub to celebrate. Later on, after a few beers, he told me that he had sold this cob several times before, but that he had always been returned as no good. He told me that each time he had taken the cob back for much less money than he had originally been paid for him. I was very puzzled as to what could have gone wrong each time. The gypsy told me that he had taken this cob to collect a load of scrap iron, but as he hadn't had the cob for long he took along his old trusted cob in case of trouble. After he had loaded the trolley up he asked the new cob to pull it home. The cob jibbed and then lay down in the road. The gypsy tied a rope around the cob's neck and hooked his old horse on to the rope. The old horse never hesitated. He wanted to go home so he dragged the young cob and trolley along the road. The cob leaped to his feet and started to pull. After that as long as he had a rope around his neck he would pull the side of a house off. If he didn't have any rope around his neck, he wouldn't pull the skin off a rice pudding.

So every time he put the horse up for sale he would put a really dirty piece of old rope around the cob's neck. Of course, the first thing the new owner did was to remove this filthy bit of rope.

There was a man who came from Minchinhampton: I seem to remember he was called Mr Samson, but I may be wrong. He used to drive a lot of different cobs. He used to deal mainly in hessian sacks that all the farmers used for grain. I haven't the faintest idea how he made this pay, but he must have done so as he was around for many years. He used to deal in most anything I think. He was one of the few who would offer helpful advice on driving horses.

The gypsies used to turn up every spring to park up down the Minety road, There was a nice bank of grass for them to graze their horses on. Again we had never seen the like of this in Devon. I always got on very well with all of them. There was an old man who only had one leg who seemed to rule the roost. His word was law with them. They told me that they were on the way from the New Forest to Evesham for the hoeing and fruit picking. They used to come back in the autumn on their way home. I could very often do a deal with them by selling them some ponies that I had broken to harness.

We milked our herd of Dexter cows a little further down the Minety road. We used to drive a cob down to these fields, tie the cows to the side of the trolley and then milk by hand, tipping the milk into the churns through a filter. One morning a wasp stung the cob and he set off at full tilt for a dewpond that was in the field, dragging the cows along with him. He came to a stop in the middle of the pond. We had to cut the little cows free before they drowned. We were in deep water trying to free the cob. He couldn't go forward because there was a fence across the pond, nor could he back the trolley out. I kept the cob calm while Sally ran to the gypsy camp. I soon heard the sound of a big horse trotting fast and Sally arrived with the gypsy cavalry. They had a harness on a big strong cob that managed to pull our cob and trolley out backwards. Time for yet another celebration in their camp that night.

One of these gypsies was trying to sell me a nice sort of coloured cob, so he took me for a drive with it. We started off nice and steady, but like all gypsies he was determined to show me how fast his cob could trot. We were flying at a rate of knots. Suddenly I realised that we were well and truly airborne. The cob had broken into a headlong gallop. The high trap that we were riding in was swaying about the road in an alarming manner. I could see that we would be ending up in the ditch. However, my driver didn't seem to be too worried. We came to a crossroads. This meant we had to cross a busy main road. *This is it!* I thought. The cob suddenly and miraculously came to an abrupt sliding halt. My driver hadn't appeared to do anything. What I hadn't noticed was that he had a piece of string that ran from his hand to the winker or blinker stays. He had simply pulled the blinkers shut right over the cob's eyes. Nothing runs very far with a bag over its eyes. Just another little trick!

One day Mr Gilbey asked me if I would mind driving a car to London for him. I hadn't a clue about finding my way about London so at first I refused to do this. However, he promised Sally and me a ride on his coach-and-four if I took the car, so of course I changed my mind very quickly. When we finally found our way to the offices in London we were invited to climb onto the coach. He had a professional coachman in charge and several other helpers. We were treated like honoured guests.

What a thrill this was. I had never ridden on a coach before. Mr Gilbey even let me drive the team for a short time on a straight quiet back street. I had never driven a team before. It was the thrill of a lifetime.

Sally and I had lunch with the directors afterwards. I wasn't so reluctant to take his car to London the next time.

I often dreamed of having a coach of my own. Realistically, I thought that this would never happen. I am happy to say that this dream has now come true. Not a very grand one, I have to admit, but nevertheless I can now boast that I own a coach and four.

Of course the driving went well for most of the time, but that would make boring reading. I have always learnt more from when things go wrong. I was gaining a lot of experience the hard way.

*

Life wasn't easy, but we were surviving, with the odd triumph along the way. What we were not prepared for was the shock of finding that the landlord was not prepared to renew our lease.

After all the work that we had put into it, we had to leave the property that was not only our home, but also our business.

CHAPTER 5

1962-1964: Moving – again and again

Having to leave our home and the stables was a terrible blow. For a while I had no idea what to do, but Mr Sebastian Gilbey kindly offered me Croft Cottage in the village, plus the use of his stables. I had to take his hunters at livery as part of the deal. That meant that we wouldn't have room for a lot of paying liveries, so the scope for income would be limited, but at least it was it was a roof over our heads.

Through the winter I used to go hunting with Mr Gilbey.

I bought a nice little black mare that a lady had been having some trouble with. I soon got her sorted out. She only needed some firm riding. I was hunting her up on the hills where she just loved jumping the walls. One day I jumped a wall only to find out, just as we took off, that there was a small quarry on the other side. It was too late to stop and we sailed out into space. It felt like an enormous drop into the bottom, but to my amazement she somehow managed to keep on her feet.

Another day while out hunting on a different part of the Cotswolds, she hit a wall very hard and cut her leg badly. I could see some roofs down in the valley so I rode down there and found what at first appeared to be a deserted and run-down manor house. I rode round it looking for any signs of life.

Suddenly an old man came out and asked me in an angry voice, "What on earth do you think you're doing riding around my house?"

I told him the mare's trouble. He came over, had a look and his manner changed completely. He took us around to his empty stables where he told me to pick up a load of cobwebs. I thought he was mad, but decided to humour him as I needed to use his phone to get help. I brought him a handful of cobwebs which he put on the wound. To my surprise the bleeding began to dry up.

Now that I understood what he wanted them for, I quickly collected lots more cobwebs. As the stables had not been used for many years there were plenty of them. We gave the mare some water and found some old hay, which she turned her nose up at. The old gentleman, who had all the appearance of an army officer of the old school, showed me into his house. There was dust and cobwebs everywhere. He showed me to an ancient telephone. To my surprise it worked. I asked Sally to bring the lorry out to fetch me. Then I realised that I didn't know where I was.

The old man told me that as his drive was overgrown I would have to walk the mare across some fields to meet Sally on the road. Having got all this organised he offered me some good malt whisky. When I was about to leave he asked me not to tell anyone that he lived there.

I duly met Sally on the road, but the odd thing was that I was never able to find the entrance to the drive and never saw this place again. Another of life's little mysteries.

We rented an old empty farmyard that was on the edge of a gravel pit. It was a ramshackle collection of galvanised iron sheds. Sally and I used it to rear calves and pigs. We built up quite a business rearing these calves. Sally would go to Gloucester, Chippenham or Cirencester market to buy them. We would grow them on big and strong so that we could resell them, hopefully at a profit.

I was running a small pigswill round in order to help with the pigs. Fred Crew farmed at Ewen about two miles away. He had a large boar, so when we thought that a sow was ready we used to walk her there along the road. One day we had taken a sow down there and all went well until we were nearly home again. The sow suddenly thought that she might like a second helping. She made a determined effort to run back to Ewen. Sally made a valiant effort to stop her, trying to head her off by shoving her bicycle in front of her. The sow shoved her head through the spokes of the front wheel. Off she went, cycle as well.

I bought a horse trailer in Cheltenham one night. It was dark. There were no lights on this trailer, but as in those days we only had to have one back light I stopped at a garage and bought a rear cycle light. When we got to Rencombe a passenger in the back of my car told me that we had lost the trailer. I thought that he was joking, but he was right.

I turned around to look for it. We came upon a group of cars parked on the side of the road. Among them was the trailer, up on the verge. I hadn't put a number plate on it. I stopped and asked what was going on. A man told me that the people with torches searching in the fields below were looking for the car that had been pulling the trailer. Then he went down to help them look. The people were so busy looking down in the fields that I managed to hook the trailer up and drove off without anyone noticing. I went home by a roundabout route.

Sally and I used to like to go to farm sales. In those days we managed to have lots of little deals, but one day she went to an Air Ministry sale and came home as proud as punch with lots of wellington boots. She wasn't so pleased when I pointed out to her they were all left-footed.

I don't enjoy farm sales so much these days. Now I'm aware that the reason the sale is taking place is because someone has died, got into trouble or it's the end of someone's dream.

*

Abbotts

I just couldn't make my efforts pay. By the end of the hunting season my finances were in a very bad shape. Breaking horses and casual work wasn't going to provide enough cash through the summer. I needed to try something different.

Very cheekily I answered an advert for a hay and straw lorry driver. I was very nervous when I went for an interview in Cirencester. I climbed up the stairs to the office and knocked on the door. A company director, Peter Ralston, greeted me. He had several bundles of different hay and straw on his desk. He asked me to identify them – which was nice and easy for me.

At the time there was no such thing as an HGV licence. I did have a clean driving licence. He asked me about my lorry driving experience. I had driven some horseboxes, Landrover and trailers and a 30cwt ex-army truck. I made as much as possible of the horsebox driving. Remember that I had learned to drive the ancient Bedford lorry when I was still a child, but I'd never driven the sorts of lorry that Abbotts used.

To my delight and astonishment he gave me the keys to a Dodge lorry and told me to go to Basingstoke to collect a load of straw, then deliver it to a pottery factory in Bristol.

I walked down to the yard where my lorry was parked. My God, she was much bigger than anything I had ever driven before. There was nothing for it but to try my luck. The lorry was a Dodge Kew with a long bonnet. It was powered by a Perkins P6 diesel engine. She was fitted with a rack that extended out over the cab, with another rack out the back to increase the carrying capacity. There were no indicators, no heaters, no power-steering and, of course, no tachographs. It was very, very noisy. I soon found out that it couldn't do much more than thirty-five mph flat out with a load on.

I was extremely nervous as I got her out onto the road. I hadn't a clue how to get to Basingstoke, so I had to stop at a roadside garage to buy a map.

I eventually found the farm that I wanted. As I drove up to it I saw to my amazement that they were still using a steam traction engine to power a threshing machine. It in turn fed straw into a stationary baler at the back. I thought that this sort of outfit had been out of use for years. The baler produced very big wire-tied bales. They really needed two men to move them about. I really had to struggle very hard to move them. As luck would have it a big strong man who was working with the thresher saw that I needed a hand. This was a real stroke of luck as he also showed me the right way to stack the bales, which is all-important. He also helped me to rope the load down. I was so grateful that I gave him a pound – a lot of money in those days.

Having got loaded, the next thing was to get out on the road and try to drive this enormous load to Bristol. As I moved down the rough farm track the lorry rolled about in a most alarming manner. I was getting more and more nervous about driving on the main road, but there was nothing for it but to get on with the job. Because of the weight of bales over the cab the steering was so very stiff. I eventually got out onto the main road and nervously put my foot down on the accelerator. I could see a big cloud of black smoke in my mirror. I was soon rolling along at about thirty miles an hour. This was nearly the top speed that this lorry could go.

The next problem was to find my way to the factory in Bristol. I had never been through Bristol before. I stopped to ask the way at a filling station as I approached the town. Fortunately they were able to give me really good directions.

Having found the pottery factory I unloaded the straw. They used it to pack china. The workers sat on the floor with a bale of straw on one side and a pile of china on the other. They were working very fast indeed, but every now and again they would throw a piece of the china against the wall, smashing it to bits. I asked them why and they said that those bits of china were cracked or misshapen.

I was so relieved to finally get out of Bristol and back to Abbotts, feeling very chuffed with myself for having managed to deliver my load safely.

I have since often wondered if I was being tested for the job. If it was a test then I must have passed, because they kept me on. For the first time in my life I was able to earn over twenty pounds a week. This was an enormous amount of money for me. I hadn't been paid when still at home, just lucky to get pocket money. In the army a private would scarcely earn more than a pound. And I had never been very good at charging my customers in the horse business; in fact, I was a hopeless businessman.

I'm still not so hot at the money side of things, but it is all different since I married Maggie. I can cope with wild horses, customers, and dealers, but forms and the like leave me in a hopeless muddle. Hard work and dangerous situations are no bother.

I was to spend the next few summers working full-time for Abbotts. In the winters I worked the lorries part-time and looked after the hunters.

Oddly enough, although I worked for Abbotts for many years, I never took another load to that pottery factory. I can remember that first day's work just like it happened yesterday.

Hay-making had just started on the Cotswolds, so I was thrown in at the deep end hauling hay all over the Westcountry and Wales.

This was the start of farmers using pick-up balers. As they hadn't much experience of working them, we often had to cope with badly baled hay. Soft bales of meadow hay were very difficult to make a load with and I had a very tough time. I worked with a co-driver who was very experienced, but either couldn't instruct or didn't want to help very much. I really struggled with these loads. It was a very tough time, but I desperately needed the money.

I used to be able to carry some three hundred bales and make a load either seven or eight bales high. The height depended on where we were going. We didn't have motorways and there were railway bridges everywhere. This was before Dr Beeching closed so many branch lines. We still sometimes had to load hay and straw onto railway trucks, but this was right at the end of using the railways for hay haulage.

Bridges were one of the main problems that I was to encounter. Every road had its share, some flat, but others made of brick arches. Most of them had signs to tell us their height, but sometimes the council had re-surfaced the road and not altered the signs. If it was one with an arch it was very important to steer for the middle. This meant that there was a great risk of meeting something coming the other way. There were several of these arched bridges on the road to South Wales after we had left Gloucester. We found out that if we drove like the clappers at them the front of the load would hit the bridge pushing down the front of the lorry. Provided we were going fast enough, we could get underneath before the tail of the lorry came up and hit the bridge. I used to play this game regularly.

We often used the A38 to Exeter and beyond. One morning I was doing this run when I came to Beam Bridge near Wellington. There was a downhill approach to it and a long uphill stretch after it, so I used to approach it as fast as possible. It was a flat bridge and I was going under it several times a week.

On this day, everything was shockingly different. The lorry hit the bridge with a tremendous bang and came to an abrupt halt, stuck firmly in the middle of the road, blocking this busy holiday route in the middle of the holiday season. The impact threw me against the steering wheel. I thought I'd broken some ribs. I was at a complete loss as to why I had got stuck. I was driving my usual lorry, the road hadn't been re-surfaced and I had the usual number of layers of bales on the lorry. What on earth could have gone wrong? Almost before I had recovered and got out of the cab, all hell was breaking loose. Angry motorists, police, ambulance, fire brigade – you name it, everybody had turned up. The lorry had gone halfway under the bridge before it got stuck. We tried to pull it clear with another lorry, but to no avail. The springs had reversed themselves under the strain. We let the tyres down, but even then we couldn't move her. We then decided, with the fire brigade's help, to try to take the top layer of bales off. This was not so easy as we had to cut the lorry tarpaulin and ropes off first. Then we had to cut the string on each bale in turn. By now the railway authorities had turned up to add their little bit. We completely blocked this busy main road for most of the day. At last we made it under the bridge leaving a huge heap of hay beside the road. A local farmer asked if he could have it: he was welcome to it. I spent hours just trying to get going again. I had to tie my ropes together as best as I could to rope up the lorry again.

I was no nearer knowing why this had happened. Next day I told the boss about it. We questioned the farmer that had supplied the load. He told us he had been using a new type of baler that he had been testing for a manufacturer. This baler was making each bale an inch higher than normal. Problem solved!

We used to haul boultings of straw. These were bundles of long straw that had been tied up at the thresher. They were not compressed, but made a lovely bed for horses. They were a proper sod to load and very difficult to rope down, as it was impossible to keep the ropes tight. Every few miles we had to stop to tighten the ropes. Unlike bales, it was very difficult to know how high the load was. I was coming home one night with such a load when I came to a railway bridge at Bourton-on-the-Water. As I tried to creep gently underneath I could feel that I wasn't going to make it. I got out and checked the height. It was no good. I had to back out and drive miles out of my way. I was very late home. I'm glad to say that I only ever hauled boultings a few times.

We were going to Lincolnshire, Norfolk, Wales and

Cornwall, working long, long hours, often sleeping in the cab or even in fields. I got back from one long run in the early hours of the morning and decided to grab a few hours sleep under the lorry. I was still asleep when the boss arrived and moved the lorry. Fortunately, I was sleeping lengthways and he drove off without running over me.

We often used what we called silent fifth gear. By this I mean we would take the lorry out of gear at the top of a hill and just let it roll down as fast as it would go. This was, of course, a very dangerous trick, but if the hill was straight and there was no other traffic about early in the morning we all used to do it.

I was coming down Shute Shelve Hill off the Mendips onto the Somerset levels and as I was running a bit late, I took the lorry out of gear. In those days there was a fairly narrow railway bridge half way down the hill. Just as I came to it a back tyre burst with a terrific bang. Then the other back tyre did the same. The lorry started to sway about all over the road. I was pushing as hard as I could on the brakes and grabbing the hand brake. None of this had much effect. As luck would have it there was nothing coming the other way. I scraped both sides of the bridge, but somehow or other I managed to keep the whole lot on the road and eventually stopped safely. Both back wheels had to be cut off with a gas torch and replaced with new wheels and tyres. I spent the whole day stuck there – so much for being just a bit late.

I never found silent fifth again!

*

There could be lots of problems getting big lorries in and out of farmyards.

One day I was taking a load of hay to a farm in Berkshire. As I came into the yard I could see some builders putting up a huge asbestos-roofed building. They had rafters sticking out of the end. I was worried that I might catch them on my load so I stopped to get somebody to watch me come in. Luckily the farmer himself decided to see me in. He was a bit impatient and he waved me on without looking carefully enough. One of the rafters stuck into the side of my load and, of course, I moved the whole roof, cracking most of the sheets of asbestos. All hell broke loose!

I was delivering a load of straw to a farm near Hereford where the straw had to be unloaded into an old stone barn. The barn had a steep ramp up to the entrance door. There was very little room to spare between the doorposts. The ramp was covered in muck and so was very slippery. I tried several times to get up this ramp, but every time the wheels started to spin. The farmer started to shout impatiently, so the next time I put my foot hard down on the accelerator. The lorry roared up the ramp only to drop down a high step in the doorway. My head hit the cab roof and my feet came off the pedals. The lorry roared straight through the barn taking out the doors and doorposts that were on the other side. I managed to stop it in a cattle yard that was covered in deep muck. The cattle panicked and smashed their way out of the yard. Then the farmer really had something to shout about!

I was trying to get into a small Somerset farm. I asked the farmer if there was room to turn in his yard. He replied that there was lots of room so I drove in. As soon as I turned in I could see that it looked nearly hopeless. The yard was very steep and covered with wet grass. As I tried to turn, the lorry started to slide across the yard. The back of the lorry swung around as if I had done a handbrake turn. By sheer chance we ended up right beside the barn that we were to unload into. The farmer couldn't believe what he had just seen. I didn't admit that it was just pure luck.

We used to go early in the morning to a café called Red Post near Newmarket. We had breakfast there while we waited for a contractor who would guide us out to a farm and help us to load. It was a run that we did fairly regularly. I remember one winter's morning we jumped out of our cabs only to slip over on the ice. We had been driving just as hard as we could to get there early. We hadn't realised how slippery the roads were.

I was loading the lorry from a rick out in a ploughed field. I got well and truly stuck trying to get out of the field. The contractor hooked a huge crawler tractor onto the back of my lorry and started to drag me backward out of the field. The load was so far out over the sides of the lorry that I couldn't use my mirrors, so I was standing on the running boards with my door open to see where I was going. The door caught on the gatepost and was ripped clean off. I somehow managed to tie on the door with some baler cord and set off for West Wales to deliver my load. This meant crossing a lot of England on a very cold winter's day, without a heater and with the wind howling in around the door all the way. It was pitch dark when I reached the farm. I was absolutely frozen. The farmer took pity on me and offered me a bed and supper for the night. Incidentally, I only ever had any offers of hospitality from smaller farmers.

In those days there was a plentiful supply of transport cafés. They varied from awful to very good. I soon learned which the good ones were.

I was working mainly in the Westcountry and Wales, but we collected hay and straw from as far away as the eastern counties and Lincolnshire. We never worked up north as Abbotts had more depots upcountry.

Sometimes I would be able to buy a lot of plums or strawberries from roadside sellers at cheap prices. Once during a miner's strike I bought a lorry load of coal from a private mine in the Forest of Dean. Sally used to take a pony and cart around selling these goods. We never made a fortune, but it was fun to do.

These are just a few more incidents that I can remember.

We were hauling straw from a huge rick on the Berkshire Downs. When we arrived there my job was to run along the thatch on the top of the rick in order to take it off. My feet went straight through the thatch and I fell down a split in the rick. I was stuck very tight between the bales, so I couldn't get out. I was shouting for help, but my co-driver couldn't see me. He eventually found me and pulled me out. It was lucky that I hadn't been working on my own or I might have been in real trouble.

I was driving out of a field that was in line with the runway at South Cerney aerodrome. It was getting dark. As I crossed an old farm bridge to get onto the road it collapsed, dropping a back wheel into the ditch. I was well and truly stuck. There were lots of learner pilots practising landing. They just skimming the top of my load. I had to wait there for a big tractor to pull me out. I just kept hoping that the pilots could see the lorry. I was very relieved when I managed to drive away home.

On another trip I had to collect bales of hay that were in among the landing lights at Fairford American Air base. This was where the bombers that were carrying the atomic bombs were based during the Cold War. I was busy putting my load on. There was a very noisy petrol elevator that was putting the bales up to me. I became aware of something behind me. It was none other than one of these enormous bombers coming in to land and only just above my head. I flung myself flat down onto the load. He was so close that I didn't think that he could miss me. Boy, he really did scare me.

We were very dependent on getting good help to load us. A good gang with pitchforks took a lot of beating as they could place the bales just right to help us. This made for a very quick loading time. Towing an elevator behind the lorry meant that each bale had to be carried the length of the lorry. If you were being loaded with a stationary elevator it was essential that the lorry bed was absolutely level as otherwise you could end up with a bad lean on the load. I learned that one the hard way!

In those far off days all our loads were loaded by hand. This meant some very hard work on a hot summer's day.

On one occasion I was loading from a field near Coates. I had a student from the Royal Agricultural College helping me to put the load on. We finished loading and he asked me how we got down to the ground. Trying to be funny I told him to shut his eyes and walk about. To my horror he did just that. He fell over the side and broke his leg. There was nobody else in the field, so I had to heave him into the cab and drive him to hospital. That made him shout a bit!

The River Severn used to flood very badly. It still does for that matter. We were given the task of delivering a load of hay to some cattle that were stranded in a farmyard that was on an island in the river valley. Two of us took the lorry to try and do this rescue mission. When we came to the flooded road we couldn't see the verges. I was the junior driver so I had to get out and wade along the road to make sure we didn't drive off the road. It was a touch-and-go operation to get to this yard, but we made it OK, although I was wet through.

I was coming home one wet and stormy night. I had delivered my load, so the lorry was empty. I had to cross the Severn. I was beginning to get very worried as the road was covered in deep water. Suddenly I saw a man standing on a gate. He was waving frantically at me, so I stopped. He told me that the bridge I was aiming for had been washed away. He had lost his car in the river. I got him into the cab and managed to back out to dry land. I was so lucky to have come across him, as I would have driven straight into the river.

They were building the Ross Spur motorway at the time. There was a real set of cowboy drivers on this job. They were all overloading and driving like madmen. We just had to try and keep out of their way. To be fair we must have been more than a bit of a nuisance to these boys with our big, slow loads.

*

I used to work on the lorries full time in the summer, but I only worked part-time in the winter as I was living in a tied cottage and was obliged to look after the landlord's horses.

I was finding keeping two jobs going at the same time very hard work, as the lorry job often meant working late into the night.

I was offered the job of being in charge of the night security at an approved school at Ashton Keynes. This was only just down the road from where we lived, so I decided to make a change and leave haulage. I found the change to working at night very difficult. I managed to stick the security job for a couple of years, but I found that it was not doing my health any good.

Meanwhile, I was still keeping some horses at livery but was unable to keep enough to make a living at it. I'm afraid to say that I was getting disenchanted with the whole scene.

*

A local farmer who did a lot of farm contracting had bought a lorry, so he and I decided to try our luck dealing in hay and straw. I gave up the security job. I had been selling hay and straw through Gloucester market on my own account and managed to do quite well out of it.

98

Having come from the Westcountry, I already had lots of connections there. Things were looking very promising. I built up a nice lot of orders; enough to keep us busy. Then, on the 23rd December 1962, a farmer from on the top of Exmoor rang me to ask if I could deliver a load of hay before Christmas. He told me that we were going to have the worst blizzard ever known. I didn't believe him. The weather looked quite settled to me, but as he was offering to pay me well, I did as he asked. I managed to find some helpers to put the load of hay on so that I would be able to make a very early start.

I arrived at the farm on Exmoor just in time for breakfast. The farmer was so glad to see me. He again told me about the snow that was coming. We got unloaded as fast as possible. I still didn't believe him. His wife gave me a hearty breakfast and I was on my way back home. As I crossed the high moor I suddenly saw snowflakes falling.

Very quickly the farmer's warning was coming true. I was having a very hairy drive home. I managed to get as far as Oaksey, but the snow was getting deeper. Just after the village there is a right-handed sharp turn. The lorry just slid sideways and crashed into a deep ditch. There was no hope of getting the lorry out. Little did I realise that it would be a couple of months before we were able to rescue it.

I managed to crawl out of the driver's window and I set out to walk the rest of the way home. The snow was up to my knees, but I only had a mile or so to go, thank goodness.

When I arrived at my home the snow had drifted up against the front door. It opened outwards, so I had to go over to the stables to get a shovel to dig myself in.

Sally had supper ready. Of course we didn't have a clue how long we would be affected, but we knew that it could be very serious for us.

During the night the snow blew under the stone Cotswold roof tiles. It settled in the attic above the bedrooms. As it melted it brought down the ceiling on top of us. That woke us up with an awful fright. In the morning everything was frozen solid. We had to dig a path to the stables to see to the horses. All of the taps were frozen, but we had enough water to boil a kettle and used it to thaw a kitchen tap. For a long time this was the only tap we could use.

We had our herd of Dexter cows at some fields near South Cerney, about three miles away. We had been milking them in a portable shed called a bail, using a milking machine. We had been using our Lambretta scooter with a sidecar fitted to it to go and look after these cows. This was useless in the snow. We had to ride two horses over there instead. The milking machine kept freezing up, so we had to milk the cows by hand.

The cold was just unbelievable. We were totally unprepared for this driving snow and cold wind. By the time we got home after each trip, we were both in an awful state.

Pigeons were falling out of the trees, dead. They were frozen stiff and so thin.

Our cottage only had one tiny open fire. This was really meant for coal, but we only had wood. It was so cold that we decided that we all had to sleep in the front room and try to keep this fire going all night. At least we had plenty of wood, even if it needed cutting up with a circular saw. As luck would have it I had been using our horse, Harry, to pull timber out of a wood.

We had a Calor gas cooker in the kitchen and a paraffin heater in the other room. We had enough paraffin at the beginning.

We were running short of churns to put the milk in as the milk lorries had all stopped running. We had to get the milk to Latton Creamery because we needed the money. I set to and made a sledge out of an old barn door. I made steel runners by cutting two steel tyres from some old waggon wheels. I heated them in an open fire and shaped them to fit the sledge.

Harry was a big strong cob who went well in harness. I put him to the sledge and off we went with Sally riding Toss Up, who had a collar and traces on in case we got stuck. The snow was blocking all the roads, so we tried to go across country. The snow was so deep and frozen so hard that we could drive over the top of the hedges. As we struggled over one hedge Harry crashed through the ice on the far side. I fell into the ditch and got soaked in freezing water, but Harry managed to drag the sledge clear and Sally caught him. The churns had fallen off, but as the milk was frozen solid it didn't spill. When we arrived at the creamery they were very glad to see us as no other milk had got there. We had to use steam hoses to thaw the milk as we needed our churns back. They very kindly found me some dry clothes to go home with. We did this trip every few days.

The weather was showing no let up at all. We made a large circle of dung in the field to exercise the horses on. We covered all the taps and pipes that we could with dung in an attempt to thaw them. We covered all the paths that we had cleared of snow with yet more dung. We even piled it up around all the doors that we weren't using in order to stop the draughts. We hung stable rugs inside the door to the house and tried to block any draughts that we could in this old cottage.

The snow blocked all the roads and cut off the village. The village shop was running out of supplies. This was very serious as all the locals did their main shopping there. There were no supermarkets or home delivery around then.

I had a tiny Farmall type A. This was an old lease-lend tractor left over from the war. It had to be started with petrol. When the engine warmed up it ran on TVO, a type of paraffin.

The local farmers couldn't start their diesel tractors because of the cold so it was up to me to try to reach Cirencester where our shop had arranged for us to pick up its supplies from a wholesaler. I had made a platform that I fixed onto the back so that I could carry as much as possible. An Air Force chap who couldn't get to work came with me.

We finally made it, but there was a long queue of people waiting to be served. I couldn't wait as it would be dark before we got home and I didn't have any lights, so I got permission to jump the queue. There were several nasty comments made at us by people in the queue.

We made it back to the shop successfully.

As luck would have it I had a large stack of firewood waiting to be cut up into logs. This turned out to be my saviour. Everybody wanted to buy firewood.

My son Stephen and a little mate asked if they could take logs around the village with our old donkey, called Gong, in a little cart. I told them not to charge the old age pensioners, as keeping warm was a matter of life and death for all of us, but even more so for them.

One morning I heard such a commotion coming from outside the yard. They had managed to get the cartwheel jammed between a telephone post and the stone wall. I had to drop everything to go to the rescue.

We didn't have the right clothing for such extreme conditions. There wasn't any chance to be able to get anywhere to buy the right gear. Just trying to get everything dry for next day was a real problem. There was no nice Gortex kit, just old ex-Army overcoats. We made puttees out of stable bandages. These worked very well to keep our legs warm.

Our supplies of hay and straw were getting very low as being so short of money we had relied on being able to buy forage as we needed it. Luckily a local farmer very kindly let us have enough on credit.

As the council didn't have much snow clearance equipment, the roads remained blocked for weeks on end. Even when they cleared a road, the wind drifted the snow back across the roads from the fields.

Trying to get home with the tractor at night, I got lost in a large field that I knew very well. I got completely disorientated in the blinding snow and the dark. I hadn't believed such a thing could happen to me. More by luck than anything I eventually found the gate. I understood how mountaineers get confused. I had crossed that field dozens of times.

Even the river that ran through the cows' fields froze over, so that we had to smash the ice every day in order for them to get a drink.

I can't remember when the weather finally changed, but it probably wasn't until April.

It was the worst winter I have ever seen in my life. I certainly hope that it is never repeated.

Ever since I have always made sure that we have enough hay, straw and firewood to see us through the winter, come what may. We always keep the tractor diesel and heating oil well topped-up for the winter.

*

If that winter of 1962-3 wasn't bad enough, life was about to get even more difficult. Mr Gilbey said that he was giving up hunting, which meant no hunters for us to look after and no need for us to be in the tied cottage with his stables.

I had the offer of a cottage and land at Duntisbourne Abbots. Very foolishly I took the lady who made this offer at her word and we moved in without anything confirmed in writing.

Once we had moved in, she completely changed her mind. This really did put us in an awful mess, but as luck would have it I met a local farmer who was desperate for help on his farm as his eldest son was away at agricultural college and his younger son was still at school. Billy Thomas really helped me out at a very difficult time of my life and I'll always be grateful. He was a good payer and provided us with a house and some land to run our stock on. We worked well together.

I had to learn a lot about modern farming. I had never driven a combine or done much baling or tractor ploughing. I did however build some of the biggest ricks that I had ever seen. I have never pretended to be a shepherd, but I used to help Billy with his Dorset Horn sheep. This flock was his pride and joy. One year he took some of these sheep to Smithfield Show leaving me to run the farm.

Billy had been suffering from farmer's lung before the show and Mrs Thomas got a call from Billy to say that he was having great trouble breathing. He had to be brought home in an ambulance. I had to drive the old farm van up to Smithfield to take over from him. When I arrived there I found to my horror that Billy hadn't managed to trim the sheep in the correct manner for the show. I hadn't a clue as to how this was supposed to be done. My luck was in, however, as I met Jack Sprague who was showing Dartmoor sheep there. Even he didn't know how these Dorset Horn sheep had to be trimmed, but he knew a man who was an expert.

We got the trimming done and I won the championship prize and got my picture in the farming press as the leading shepherd!

I bought a pony for sixpence in a pub one night. The owner's children had tied the pony up to the downpipe of some roof guttering. The pony backed away and tore the guttering off the roof. He galloped madly away dragging the metal guttering behind him. He was now so terrified and nervous that he was proving useless. The owner seemed happy to agree that the pony would never be any good again and he gladly accepted my offer just to get the pony off his hands.

He turned out to be a really nice pony after I had spent a lot of time getting his confidence. I spent a long time long reining him. Then I soon got him in harness and pulling a little cart about. I was able to use him to collect empty paper farm feed sacks. I used to collect these sacks in my spare time, haul them home and store them in an old shed. When I had filled the shed I got a friend who had a Landrover and trailer to take them to a factory near Stroud. Later, my son Stephen and my daughter Honor rode Sixpence when I was not using him for the sacks.

I was driving a Ferguson that had a fore end loader fitted to it. I was coming out of the farm drive onto the main Cirencester to Gloucester road when a car shot across in front of me. To my horror I found that I had collected a suitcase case full of ladies undies from the roof rack on the end of the loader. I duly took them into the police station. They had a good laugh about it.

I was ploughing beside this same road later on that winter. I didn't have a cab, so I was getting very cold. Suddenly I thought I could see some bank notes blowing about in the field. I couldn't believe my eyes. I stopped and did a check. Sure enough there were notes of all different values blowing about in the wind. I forgot all about the ploughing and roared off home to get Sally to help me catch these notes before they blew away.

We kept them for a long time, but nobody reported them missing. Was it the receipts of a robbery? It was a great help for us at a very bad time. Manna from heaven.

I used to have to look after our cows and ponies after I had finished work on the farm. That meant I was working by a Tilley lamp a lot in the winter. One night I was coming home along the main road with a load of hay on a cart that was being pulled by a big donkey that I had bought at Stow Fair. I was carrying my lantern. A police car pulled up and the constable accused me of stealing the hay.

He ordered me to take it home, then he took me to the

police station. When I arrived the sergeant in charge knew me well. I explained what I had been doing and where the hay had come from. He gave the young constable a dressing down and told him to take me home.

Billy's son had finished at agricultural college, so Billy didn't need us to help on the farm anymore. He was happy for us to stay on in the cottage, but I needed to find work. We were determined to own a place of our own, so I needed something that paid enough for us to build up some capital – and Sally was expecting our second child.

I went back to driving lorries. I got a job with P & S Lorries who delivered bathrooms all over the country. It meant long hours and being away from home a lot, but I was earning more money than I'd ever earned before.

Our daughter, Honor, was born on the 15th October 1964.

Shortly afterwards we saw a newspaper advertisement for an auction where one of the lots was forty acres of land on the Cotswold escarpment overlooking Cheltenham racecourse. We went along to have a look at it, although we thought it was bound to be out of our price range. The lady owner obviously thought so too as she was more than a bit snotty.

The land was completely neglected. There were almost no fences, no house or buildings and, more importantly, no apparent water supply. It was for the most part very steep and a lot of it was covered in thorn trees. It must have looked completely useless to most people.

I did, however, ask an old timer who was drinking in the local pub if he knew if there was any water on this land. To my surprise he told me that many years ago there had been a spring that fed into a stone trough. We went back up there and managed to find a damp patch of ground hidden underneath a huge patch of brambles. We dug it out and did indeed find the old trough that still had a trickle of water feeding into it. This solved the main problem with this land.

We still thought we'd never be able to afford it, so we didn't bother going to the auction. A few days later the auctioneer called at our cottage to tell us that they had failed to sell the land at auction.

We had one thousand pounds saved up in a tin. We didn't

even have a bank account. We offered them this money. To our amazement they said that if we found another £100 we could have the land. So the deal was done. We were both so excited to finally own our own land. We bought an old caravan for ten pounds and towed it over there, hiding it under some trees.

We told Billy that we would be leaving his cottage, but we had one last bit of fun before we left.

When we'd moved in we'd known that Billy's cottage had woodworm and we had moved in with some very cheap furniture that we wouldn't mind becoming infested. We wouldn't have use for it in the caravan so we decided to scrap the lot. As the cottage had a spiral staircase it was going to be a lot of trouble to get anything down the stairs. I took my chainsaw and axe upstairs and started smashing the furniture to bits and throwing it out of the window.

Sally always had an odd sense of humour. When a neighbour went by she shouted that I had gone mad and was breaking up the happy home. The neighbour promptly rang the police who sent a squad car to investigate. The next thing I was aware of was a very nervous policeman peering up the stairs. We had a good laugh about that one.

Our spell in Duntisbourne was over. It was time to move on.

CHAPTER 6

1964-1973: Cheltenham; our first house; buying Stinhall

Now we owned forty acres of unfenced, derelict hillside, largely covered in thorn trees – and we shared it with a large family of badgers. The caravan hidden in the trees wasn't very legal, but we got away with it for years.

Through the week I was driving lorries all over the country and saving my 'night out' money by sleeping in the lorry. I spent all Sunday fencing. After some time I managed to get part of the land stockproof. It took a lot longer to fence right around the outside. I dug out the area around the old water trough and cleaned it up. Water trickled steadily into it. So I was solving two of the problems.

They were building the M5 past Cheltenham at the time and I met an Irish lad who worked on the project with his own huge bulldozer. He offered to come and clear any thorns that we wanted shifting.

He cleared the whole lot in a day, apart from those around the caravan, and swept it all up into a huge heap as big as a house. It stayed there for the rest of the summer. November the fifth arrived. Sally's brother, Colin, and his children came down from London and we decided to have an enormous bonfire.

I put a lot of straw and tyres around the heap; heaved several gallons of paraffin over the whole lot and dropped a match onto it. With a roar the flames shot high into the night. In fact I had to run like hell to get away from it. As we were high on the escarpment above Cheltenham the blaze could be seen for miles. I must admit that I never thought of anyone ringing the fire brigade. Suddenly we could see the lights and hear the sirens, all heading our way. The lane from Prestbury became more track than road long before our bottom gate, but some firemen managed to reach us. We had a real party going by then with friends and neighbours. The firemen took it well: maybe the bottles of homemade cider we gave them helped.

*

Peter was a Dartmoor pony I bought on a trip to Chagford Pony Fair. He was only a foal, but he was to stay with us for the rest of his life. I broke him to ride and drive. He was only about eleven hands high, but was a great character. My daughters learned to ride on him.

On one occasion, when she was still tiny, my daughter Honor asked to be let off the lead. I thought she would be all right walking slowly, so I let her go. To my horror she clapped her heels into him and shot off up the track. I could hear her squeals, but couldn't do anything about it. I was running after them, but couldn't catch up. As luck would have it the gate was shut at the end of the track and they stopped.

When I reached her I realised that, not only was she all right, but she had a big grin all over her face. Was I relieved!

As I was away with the lorry so much I didn't see enough of my children.

The day of Prestbury Show dawned and I was at home for it. Honor wanted to take Peter and have a go in the showjumping. She seemed so small to me that I wasn't at all sure about this. I said that if she could jump a canteen type bench we had, she could go. She turned Peter around and cantered him at it. He flew over it and she stayed on board – so off to the show we all went.

There was such a kind lady running the jumping. Honor was by a long way the youngest competitor. Her feet didn't come below the saddle flaps. I was very nervous about her, but she and Peter just flew around. They did a clear round, much to my surprise – and relief. I was terrified and proud in equal measure. If I remember right, she was second that year and won it the following year.

I used Peter in a little cart that Sally had made from a scrap car trailer. I was using him to take around the fencing tools and materials. He would happily stand about eating grass while I was busy with the fencing. However, one day some ramblers left a gate open with the result that other horses galloped into the field that we were in. Of course, Peter joined in the fun and galloped off after them taking the cart with him. They shot along a track that ran above a small quarry. The wheel of Peter's cart went over the edge. The cart toppled over and dragged Peter with it. They rolled all the way down the sloping side of the quarry and finished up with both Peter and the cart the right way up and apparently no worse for the experience.

Peter had another fright with a second sand and gravel quarry we had on this land. The quarry was on a very steep hill. I would take Peter up there and put a load of gravel on the sledge. The sledge took very little pulling down the hill, but one morning I made an early start and it was frosty. As Peter turned down the hill the sledge took off. It swept Peter's back legs away and he sat down on the sledge like a dog. He shot off down the hill. I could only watch in horror. To my utter relief he stayed upright and ended up in the yard I was putting the gravel in. He looked a bit surprised, but was quite all right.

I remember Peter and Honor getting into trouble with a well-known local racehorse trainer. They thought it would be fun to gallop past the string of racehorses. They managed to wreak quite a bit of havoc. The trainer was not amused and he told me so rather plainly. I believe Pat Eddery was an apprentice there at the time.

*

I was driving many thousands of miles a year delivering baths and when you do that many miles you have to expect your fair share of incidents. Here are a few that I remember.

I was working all hours. Heading home in the early hours of the morning I felt too tired to go on and I pulled into the gateway of a redundant railway station. I must have fallen asleep as I was pulling up. I was woken by another of our drivers, who was on early start, blowing his horn as he went by. I woke to find a hedge right in front of me and the engine still running. I frantically jammed my foot on the brakes, but of course I was already parked. It gave me an awful fright.

Early one morning I set off to the south coast. As I passed Boscombe Down I saw a strange looking thing flying beside

109

me. I had never seen anything like it. I told the other drivers when I got back, but nobody would believe me. It turned out to be the Flying Bedstead, the forerunner of the Harrier jump jet.

They were building the M4 and M5 at this time. What a great day it was when they joined them together in Birmingham, allowing us to get home more quickly. These roads seemed huge to us: we thought that they would never fill with traffic. How wrong we were.

I was coming out of Hull, heading for home, when I saw a large artic lying on its side in a ditch. The driver waved me down and I stopped to help. I gave him a lift to the nearest phone. To my astonishment he told me that he had been deliberately run off the road by another lorry. I asked him why anyone would do such a thing. He told me that there was trouble in the Hull fishing fleet and some protesters were trying to stop any freezer lorries from leaving Hull. I was finding it hard to believe him.

I looked in my mirrors and to my horror I could see a large tipper lorry trying to pass me at speed. As he swept by, he tried to force me off the road. As I had been warned, I slammed on my brakes very hard with the result he overshot me and crashed into the ditch himself. I put my foot down on the floorboards and got the hell out of it. I dropped the other driver in Goole.

In hindsight, my lorry was fitted with a Rollalong container that could have been taken for a freezer lorry.

On another occasion I was driving from Grimsby to Hull before the Humber Bridge had been built, which meant a long drive up to Goole to get across the river. I was following a six-wheeled tipper lorry that was overloaded with chippings piled very high. He was driving very fast and as he swept around some of the sharp corners I could see the chippings being flung off. I was thinking that this driver must be some young cowboy and that I had better not get too close as I felt he might well wrap it all up. We were held up at a level crossing, so I thought I would go and have a quick friendly chat with this driver. To my astonishment he was an older driver, sitting in his cab puffing away at his pipe. I certainly got that one wrong.

I got lost on Biddulph Moor, just north of Stoke-on-Trent. It came on to snow quite hard and quickly covered the roads. I came to an isolated crossroads only to find that the sign post had been broken off and was lying in the snow. I hadn't a clue as to which was the right road to go down. I suddenly spotted a man walking towards me. *Thank God for that,* I thought, *directions!* Just my luck – he was a foreigner and didn't speak a word of English. I always carried a shovel during the winter and was able to scrape the snow away to find the road markings which helped me find the main road.

On another day I was delivering in Stoke when, as I reached the brow of a hill, I could see a very low bridge in front of me. I realised that it looked too low for my lorry. I got lots of warning flashes and I caused chaos by reversing a long way against the traffic.

I was driving just outside Ashford in Kent and I certainly wasn't hanging about as we had to cover a lot of ground to earn a living, but as I slowed down for some nasty bends a huge petrol tanker swept past me. He must have realised that he was in trouble. I saw his brake lights come on and smoke pour from his tyres. He crashed into some trees and exploded with an enormous bang. I managed to stop before I ran into the wreckage, but the force of the explosion blew my windscreen out.

I was unloading in a back street in Bedford. As I passed a bath off the back of the lorry, the storeman was distracted by something. I tried to hang on to the bath, but it went over the point of balance and I fell out onto the road. I swore loudly at the stupid storeman who ran away and didn't come back. I was in agony, but managed to drag myself back into the lorry cab. I drove on to Red Post Café outside Newmarket. When I arrived there I couldn't get out of the lorry. I had to attract the attention of another driver. He was so good and called an ambulance. I had broken a bone in my leg – no wonder it hurt a bit!

I was approaching a set of traffic lights. There were two cars in front of me. The front one stalled when the lights changed so the driver, who was an elegant lady, got out and tried to start it with a starting handle, but with no success. The man in the other car started blowing his horn. The infuriated lady came back to his car and brought the starting handle down across the bonnet of his smart car with a terrific crash.

She shouted at him, "You swing the ******* handle and I'll blow the ******* horn." She had frightened the life out of him and he shot off. I had a job to stop laughing, but I gave her a hand to get started.

I was heading towards Swindon when a big milk tanker pulled out in front of me. He went off towards Swindon as fast as he could go, but he had a long pipe hanging from the rear of his lorry. It was thrashing wildly about with milk still pouring from it. I couldn't pass him and it took a lot of light flashing before he looked in his mirrors. The creamery was run by the Co-op and as such was a union place. Drivers used to back up to the unloading bay and the rest was up to the dairy workers who, when they had finished, would bang on the side of the tanker. This time some joker saw that the driver was fast asleep and banged on the side of his cab. He'd woken up, slammed it into gear and shot off!

*

Sally's mother died and left her just enough money to buy a little cottage at the top of Aggs Hill. It was the first house we had ever owned and we were thrilled to bits. It had a big garden and a fantastic view over Cheltenham, Gloucester down the Severn Vale, and away to the Malverns.

It was within walking distance of our land. It would have been better if it was closer, but it was the nearest property that was available and that we could afford.

That first night we celebrated by having fish and chips washed down with some champagne that I had taken in a deal.

I had a bad fall off a horse and I became temporarily partly paralysed below the waist. I refused to stay in hospital. Sally made me up a bed downstairs, but I couldn't get out of it without assistance. I was lying there one afternoon when Peter, who was meant to be tied up outside waiting for Honor to come home from school, got free and pushed his way into the house. The door slammed behind him so that I couldn't chase him out. He found a loaf of bread on the table and swept it about with his teeth. He wrecked the front room. Sally was not best pleased.

In the garden we had a tall old ash tree that was rotten. I was afraid that it would blow down, so I made inquiries about having it felled. The quotes we got were far more than we could afford. One night I met a man in a pub at Charlton Kings who told me he had been a lumberjack in Canada. He said he loved doing a tree that was a challenge. He also gave me the name of somebody that he had done several jobs for. I checked this out and then asked him to come and help me. He duly turned up and put two pegs in the ground telling me that if he didn't get the tree to fall between the pegs I wouldn't owe him anything. He eyed the tree up and down, started his chainsaw and dropped the tree exactly where he had said he would.

Sally gave birth to Clare, our third child, but there were complications and I had to stop work to look after her and the growing numbers of stock.

We had just bought some Gloucester cows from an old farmer down in the Berkeley Vale. We bought them because of their white tails and white stripe down their backs, which would make them easier to see when we went to milk the cows after dark. The little black Dexters were very difficult to see at night.

A few months later a sale was held of Gloucesters in the Vale. It attracted a lot of attention from the media and it looked as if we'd get a good price if we sold our cows. They did make a lot of money. The old farmer was not very happy. I believe that this was the start of the Rare Breeds movement.

I bought a lot of treetops that had been left after the timber people had felled a wood several miles from our house. If anyone thinks that cutting up logs and selling them is a way to get rich, just forget it. I did, as usual, have one nasty moment. The wood was several miles from our house. I had loaded a farm trailer with logs, but for some reason I hadn't brought it home. I went off on the Fordson Major tractor to collect it. We had had a very hard spell of frost. It was dark. As I tried to hook up the trailer it slipped off the blocks holding the draw bar up and crashed down onto my foot. I only had wellington boots on and the pain was awful, but worse was still to come. I couldn't get my foot free. I was miles from anywhere and worse still nobody knew where I was. Then it started to snow. The ground was frozen solid and it looked like I might be trapped until someone found me. I just managed to reach a tool box on the back of the tractor and found a spanner with which I scraped at the frozen ground under my foot. It took a long time, but eventually I was able to pull my foot out of the boot. I was so relieved to get back on the tractor, but it had no cab, it was freezing cold and I had a bare foot with several miles to drive home.

The winter passed and Sally had got better, so I took an early morning job driving a lorry delivering thirds of a pint of milk around all the schools in Cheltenham.

I had a West Indian mate called Keith who had come to this country as an immigrant. I had never worked with a black man before, but we got on all right and I learned a lot about colour and its problems. Keith was a good mate and we became friends. He had done the job as driver's mate for years. He couldn't drive and he couldn't read.

We also used to take unsold skimmed milk out to farms for pig food. The milk had to be tipped into a big open tank. We were doing this one cold morning when there was ice everywhere. Keith was showing me how to tip the churns quickly. I warned him about the ice, but as I was speaking he slipped into the tank of smelly milk. I pulled him out, but I wasn't going to let him back into my cab smelling like that. It wasn't far to his home and he rode on the outside while I drove there.

He was married to a white girl and they had several small children. Keith thought the world of them. One morning he came to work in a terrible state. He told me that his wife seemed to have left him and he didn't know where she had gone. He had a letter in his hand, but he couldn't read it. I read it for him and found it was a letter offering his wife a job at a very up-market country hotel.

As there was no bus service to it, I agreed to take Keith up there. We took the children with us. When we arrived we found it was indeed very grand. I thought that it might be wiser if I went into the hotel first and made enquiries. I met a very attractive, if rather snooty, manageress who was very evasive. I couldn't get a straight answer, but I felt certain that his wife was working there.

Time to put the terrier in to bolt her!

I told Keith to take all his small children into the hotel and tell this snooty manageress that she could look after them. It worked. Within minutes the family was reunited.

Sally had fully recovered and we felt that I could again be away from home more. We were also desperate for more money, so I took a job as a long-distance lorry driver with Oldacres, who were an animal feed merchants in Bishops Cleeve. They were very much an ambitious company, growing day-by-day. The money was good, but they really wanted an enormous amount of work to earn it.

I was given the area from Bishops Cleeve westwards into Wales. I was driving an old Commer two-stroke lorry. These lorries were fast and had a distinctive wailing engine note. They were a joy to drive and didn't easily get stuck in the farm mud.

I got on well with the Welsh farmers. We had to deliver feed stuff come hell or high water. That's just what we did, as there was a good spirit in the firm. One day I reached Builth Wells in a blizzard, but got stuck trying to go up the mountain to some farms. I rang a farmer and told him the position. He brought down a huge forestry bulldozer and towed me to the top of the mountain. He had rung the other farmers and they met us on a windswept crossroads. I got unloaded as quickly as possible – not so easy with the snow cutting my face and my hands freezing.

I left the depot early one morning with a load for Wales. I made some calls then as I went uphill there was a sound from the engine that I took to be the dynamo about to pack up. I just ignored it and hoped it would go away, but it was still doing it when the lorry was empty and I was on the way home. I stopped in a lay-by for a break and thought that I had better take a look, even though I didn't know much about mechanics. I got the floorboards up so that I could see into the engine. I was horrified to find a tiny kitten trapped against the exhaust manifold. I got him out, but he was terribly burnt along his side. As luck would have it, I knew a vet not far away. I had the kitten treated and then took him back to the yard. He lived there happily for many years, but he never grew much hair on that side, neither did he get into lorries again!

I was coming back from Wiltshire one night. I stopped at a pub for a drink and met a man I knew there. He told me that there was an old horse farm wagon for sale next door. The lady who owned it said she was sorry to sell it as it had been in the family for generations, but she was moving out and it had to go it. I made a deal with her and we got some men to help us load it on the lorry. I unloaded it at home before returning to the depot.

When I got in for work the next day there was a note for me to see the manager. He wanted to know how long we had been in the wagon haulage business. All I could do was plead guilty, but he made nothing of it.

I found out later that this wagon was an old stage wagon. It was a double-shafted wagon that had been pulled by six horses from Minety to London and back. I showed it at the Devon County Show in the early seventies. It was constructed just like the Conestoga wagons. As has been quite usual in my life, funds ran short so it had to go.

*

It was about this time that my father died.

The family home farm of Stiniel and the nearby farm of Stinhall, where Jack Sprague was still the tenant, were divided up into a number of lots to be sold at auction.

Father's solicitors handled all the arrangements, but they were very unforthcoming about the size of the estate. I knew that my sister and I were the only beneficiaries. There were assets to be sold, but Father had run up a lot of debts. He never had any idea about money and would never discuss it. There had always been money in his family and he just seemed to be convinced that it would always be there to spend.

When I was down in Devon I called into the local pub. As soon as she saw me the barmaid flew into a rage. I had no idea what she was ranting about, but when I'd calmed her down she explained that she had heard my sister talking with a group of people. She said they were planning on buying Stinhall and pressuring Jack Sprague to get out so that they could sell it on at a profit. She had assumed that I must be in on it, but it was the first I'd heard of it.

I realised that it would suit me very well to buy Stinhall – not for then, but for some time in the future. I liked the idea of returning to Devon, even if it wasn't until retirement. I also

116

didn't like the idea of old Jack being forced out of his home. But, of course, I didn't have any money to buy it.

As I thought about it a plan began to form. I'd had details of the auction and Stinhall was to be the last lot sold. I looked at the guide prices of the other lots. If they all sold for a lot more than the guide price, then my half might be enough to buy Stinhall – depending on the size of the debts that had to be settled from the estate. I wasn't sure about the legality of bidding at auction when I didn't have the money to pay, so I talked it through with my own solicitor. He said that it was unconventional and not something he wished to encourage, but from a practical point of view it might just work. After all, what could Father's solicitors do? They could either accept the situation and sort out the estate on the basis of what I'd done, or they could organise another auction and put Stinhall up for sale again.

I arranged for an auctioneer friend of mine from the Cotswolds to attend the auction and bid on my behalf, so that no one would know that it was me who was trying to buy it. We sat on opposite sides of the room and I told him to keep bidding until I got up and walked out. I made a note of the prices made by all the other lots and did my calculations.

I was very nervous through the bidding for Stinhall, but just before my limit was reached the hammer came down and it was sold to my auctioneer friend. I had bought Stinhall. All I had to do was pay for it. Father's solicitors were furious when they found out what I'd done, but they let it go through.

My calculations were out. The debts were bigger than I'd guessed and I had to borrow some money to complete the purchase.

Sally was furious when she found out what I'd done. Instead of receiving an inheritance, I'd got into debt buying a farm that she didn't want.

But as tragedy was to strike our family in the not too distant future, buying Stinhall turned out to be a blessing.

*

The excitement of the auction over, life continued.

Owning land close to a town made us a target for rubbish dumpers. One day I saw two people throw some rubbish over our gate and drive off in a smart sports car. I grabbed the bags of rubbish and jumped into my truck. I saw them turn into a housing estate and pull onto a nice smart drive. I roared up behind them and chucked the contents of the bags all across the lawn. They found somewhere else to dump their rubbish after that.

We still kept some pigs. We could get waste bread from the bakery, skimmed milk from the dairy and some waste animal feed from Oldacres, so they didn't cost much to feed.

I bought an Austin Champ, a type of jeep that the Army used. It would go backwards nearly as fast as forwards. It was very powerful and would go almost anywhere across country. I used it to carry dynamite across country for a contractor friend who blew up tree stumps, or anything else he was paid to remove. I was nervous about doing it, but he paid well. I just learned to keep well out of the way when he was setting the fuses. Give me a wild horse to deal with, any day.

We had a Dexter bull that was a nice gentle character – until a dog appeared. We had trouble with trespassers, in spite of notices stating that the land was private. I was calling the bull towards the gate when I found a group of people climbing over it, although it was locked and had a warning notice saying, 'Beware of the Bull'. They had a dog with them. I advised them that the bull was coming along the track they intended to use. They told me to get lost and climbed over the gate, in spite of my warnings. They weren't far into the field when the bull appeared. The bull saw the dog, lowered his horns and with a great bellow charged them. I leapt over the fence for my own safety. They only just got out in time – and then they tried to blame me!

We had a Jack Russell terrier that just loved to go to ground. He vanished one day. Sally and I both thought that he must be stuck in an earth somewhere. We all walked miles searching for any trace of him. We were just about to give up the search when a whippet I had with me kept going back to the same bit of ground. He was pointing with his nose and digging at something, but was a long way from any earth. I started digging and the deeper I dug, the more excited the whippet got. I dug down well over two feet – and found the terrier. He was really stinking, but otherwise OK. We were delighted to have him back and he seemed just as pleased to see us.

The cottage was just too far from our land to be convenient. We decided to try to get planning permission to build on our land on agricultural grounds. We thought it would help if we were already living there, so we bought a second caravan and put it alongside the first one. Then we sold the cottage and moved into the caravans – with no mains services or telephone.

*

I was still driving for Oldacres. More than my fair share of accidents seemed to come my way. I wasn't personally involved in that many, but I witnessed some that really shook me up, and some that made me smile. Thinking about it, it's surprising that I wasn't involved in more. We worked too long hours, were encouraged to break all the regulations and I was frequently over-loaded. The pursuit of money was all that mattered.

I was coming home one night with the lorry when I came upon a big car stuck in a ditch. A man waved me down and asked me if I could pull him out. I managed to get a rope tied onto his car. Then I realised that there were people still in it. I suggested that it would be better and safer if they got out. He seemed a bit reluctant, but I insisted. Well out they got, and I could see why he was being cagey. There were five or six girls squeezed into the car and I didn't have to be the Brain of Britain to work out what their occupation was.

I got the car back on the road. The driver was very generous and then asked the way to a farm I knew well. We had all been wondering how that particular farmer had been able to buy new cars and gear as he had been letting the farm go to rack and ruin for years. All was now revealed, especially as we then became aware of all the cars heading that way at night.

We used to take animal feed to Carmarthen in West Wales. As it was such a long trip two of us would go so we could take turns at the driving. A young man who played the guitar well often came as my co-driver. In fact he played his guitar most of the time. We had a brand new Dodge lorry that was fitted with a Cummins V8 engine. It was by a long way the fastest lorry that I ever drove. It was nose heavy when it was empty and liable to skid if I got it wrong. One night I had to brake heavily at a roundabout outside Ross-on-Wye. The lorry just went straight on, right over the top of the roundabout, taking signs with it and severely frightening us. Luckily, nobody else was about.

I had an accident outside Tetbury when a car came round a bend right on my side of the road. I swerved to avoid him, but he hit the front of my lorry and crashed through the hedge on the other side of the road. I went through a stone wall and ended up on somebody's lawn. The owner was a retired colonel and not best pleased. I was grateful for the long bonnet of the lorry and glad to be alive.

Someone backing a car out onto the main road caused one shunt that I had at Castle Eden in the north of England. The lorry in front of me ran into them. I'd been following the lorry at a safe distance, but had complete brake failure. I had to run into the back of the lorry, as there was another lorry coming towards me. Again, the long bonnet saved me. It turned out that a fitter had put the brake back together incorrectly.

I witnessed an awful smash when a lorry burst a front tyre and cut a coach in two, lengthways. It took me a long time to get over that one, although I was not directly involved.

Driving into Hereford one dark evening, a furniture lorry came towards me and as we drew level his back door swung open and smashed into my lorry breaking the windscreen and making a real mess of the cab. I crashed into the front of some houses. Luckily, nobody was hurt, but I was more than a bit shocked.

Coming back across the Severn Bridge I noticed smoke coming into my cab from the engine. As there was a hefty charge for being towed off the bridge I put my foot down, charged the tolls, pulled into the side, grabbed my dinner bag and coat and jumped out as fast as possible. Almost as soon as I hit the road the lorry exploded in a sheet of flame. Once again I had got away with it.

I was thinking that my guardian angel was always going to be there, but then all my share of bad luck came at once.

120

CHAPTER 7

Tragedy and return to Devon

This was to prove the most difficult time in my life. Looking back on it now, I cannot understand how I coped, with almost no help at all. I suppose I had no choice – I just had to cope somehow.

I took Honor and Clare out riding one Sunday morning. When we got home we found the fire brigade and an ambulance on our land. Our tractor was on its side, having come off the track. Poor Sally was being lifted into the ambulance.

I was told that some youths had set fire to an area of wasteland that adjoined our boundary. We had a big rick of straw close to the fence. No one knew for sure, but it looked as if Sally had realised the danger to the straw. She was a capable tractor driver, so she'd driven the tractor, which happened to have a plough attached, up the track, maybe with the idea of ploughing a firebreak. I can only think that the smoke hid the track for a moment and a wheel left the track. However it had happened, the tractor had turned over and crushed her. Stephen had somehow got the tractor off her and raised the alarm.

I followed the ambulance to Cheltenham Hospital. Sally was still alive when we got there. I had to wait what seemed a very long time until a doctor came out and told me that she had died.

I walked out of the hospital in a daze and then had to tell my children the awful news.

We had just got through the funeral when I got a tip-off from a good friend that social services intended to put my children into care. They must have seen the caravans and decided they weren't going to leave three children to live there with just a man on his own to look after them and earn a living. There was absolutely no way I was going to let that happen. I

121

promptly loaded them into the Landrover and took them to a good friend of mine in Devon.

Stephen wanted to go to agricultural college. It was a condition that students had to put in at least a year of practical farm work before going to college. He was old enough to leave school and I arranged for him to go to the farm of Mr and Mrs Courtier of North Tawton, where he stayed until he went to Bicton.

I told Margaret Andrews of Weddicott Farm, who was looking after Honor and Clare, that I wasn't going to send them to any school until I had got us properly sorted out – I didn't want social services tracing us.

Jack Sprague was getting on a bit, but he was still the tenant of Stinhall and running his flock of sheep. I called in for a chat. When he heard the position that we were in he made me a very kind offer. He pointed out that there was plenty of room in the farmhouse for all of us and he invited me and the children to move in with him.

This was the only option open to me as far as I could see. There really didn't seem to be anywhere else for us to go. And it had the advantage that when I'd bought Stinhall at auction it had come with some land and buildings that were not in the tenancy, so I'd be able to do something – although I wasn't sure what that something would be.

I returned to the Cotswold caravans, sold as much stock as I could and found a buyer for the land, which gave me a small amount of capital. Social services were trying to track us down and one of the staff caught up with me. She was on the receiving end of some very harsh words from me, but I did learn that if they knew the girls were living in a proper house and had a woman involved in looking after them, they would get off my back.

I'd met a girl called Liz who was keeping her horse at livery on the next door farm, owned by Mr & Mrs Fry. She had trained as a teacher, but hadn't yet got into teaching. She had suffered a similar tragedy to mine, and at almost the same time. Her brother had fallen out of a train and been killed. We were both in a state, neither of us knowing what we were going to do with ourselves. She needed somewhere to keep her horse, but couldn't afford to pay for livery.

Liz was brave enough to come to Devon with us. She didn't know much about bringing up children, but we worked together to set up a home for us all.

The old farmhouse didn't have electricity, but had running water and flush toilets.

As I had been self-employed at the time of Sally's death and had a small amount of capital, I didn't seem to qualify for any financial help from the State. As far as I was concerned the important thing was to try to do my best for the children in what was a very difficult time for them. I really didn't want to return to full-time lorry driving and be away from home so much.

In the next two years I spent as much time as possible with Honor and Clare and we went to a lot of shows and gymkhanas with their ponies. I picked up some casual lorry driving and farm work whenever I could fit it in with their being at school. I didn't have enough land, or capital, to be farming on my own account. Then I got a part-time postman's job in Chagford. It was good to have a more regular income, even if it wasn't much. I was also doing a bit of pony trekking on the moor.

We'd been together for several years and we seemed to be getting on well as a family, so Liz and I decided to get married.

Shortly afterwards, Jack Sprague passed away.

*

Many years before, Arthur Palmer, who was then the farrier at Chagford, had taught me to shoe horses. I had not done a lot to this while I was on the Cotswolds, but when I returned to Devon I couldn't find anyone who would take our work on at a reasonable price. I found Arthur, who had retired because he was very crippled by arthritis. He was delighted to come and help me, even if all he could do was sit in a chair and advise. I put a nice comfy chair in the forge and he gave me the benefit of all his years of experience.

Various people started coming in for freebie advice on horsey matters. While I was happy to give it, it didn't help my bank balance. Because they had known my father, they seemed to think that I must have money.

One source of income was taking people out riding on the moor. The trekking was never my favourite occupation, but it has provided useful income. A large number of the customers had almost no riding experience, even if they had claimed they could ride. Maybe they'd sat on a rocking horse as a small child! Often the 'trekking' turned into a riding lesson.

Teaching a rising trot was almost impossible when we only had them for an hour, with very little chance that we would ever see them again anyway. I was at a party one night and talking to an up-market old lady. She asked how we were getting along with the riding and I mentioned the trotting problems. To my surprise she told me that she found it was an easy thing to teach, so I asked her what she did. She told me to get them mounted then make them catch hold of the neck strap and practise rising up and down in the stirrups while the horse was standing still. Having got them doing that, she told me to get them to follow me down the road at a walk with them still going up and down. She then told me to shout, "Trot on."

She said that the horses would trot on and put themselves in time with the riders. I didn't believe it, but if the people were prepared to try it, it worked a treat. The trick was not to trot too far, and to keep stopping to let them recover. It most certainly worked. Nobody was more surprised than I was.

I had a German couple come who wanted me to give them a guided tour of as many of the ancient burial sites and other Bronze Age remains as I could. They could both ride and we had a pleasant week exploring Dartmoor.

One day we rode over the top of Hambledon Hill. The man asked, "What are all those tall poles for that are sticking out of the ground?"

My brain must have been out of gear as, without thinking, I replied, "Oh, that's to stop the bloody Germans back in the war."

Luckily they had a good laugh, but I must say I felt most awkward.

A Dutch couple, William and Ina, were running a guest house near us and naturally they had mostly Dutch people staying there. They were really nice people. We all had such a lot of fun with them.

One group said that they would like to go out for "zee foxhunting", so I arranged with the South Devon Hunt that I would take them out cub hunting at Spitchwick Park. It was very early on a bright autumn morning. I had three people riding, but a large number of bearded and rather arty-looking supporters. I had to explain who they were, as the Huntsman thought they were an anti-hunt group. They all had a nice morning in this lovely park. I don't think any foxes were killed, as the hounds were mostly puppies. In fact, it very often looked as if the foxes might be chasing the hounds! The Dutch people said it made them feel very grand as in Holland only the Royal Family and their friends hunted.

I later went over to Holland with them. It was the first time I had ever been abroad. They looked after me and took me to Ina's father's farm out on the polder. I was surprised that they still kept cows in the lower part of the farmhouse, just as they did many years ago at home. The fog was so thick that I never saw much of the countryside.

They took me into Rotterdam and said we had to take a lift to get to the bar. We all got in. My tummy gave a terrific lurch, but the lift soon stopped. I got out and Ina led me over to the window. To my astonishment we were hundreds of feet above the ground. I am terrified of heights, so I rushed over to the bar to pour some courage down my throat! I believe the tower was called the Euromast.

We went to a shop where you could buy cheap harness off the shelf. That was a real surprise for me. They also had a selection of modern carts for sale. At that time there wouldn't have been anywhere like it in England or, if there was, I hadn't heard of it.

They took me to a party the like of which I had never been to. The booze was free and gallons of it. I asked Ina how we were going to get home as I could see our driver was absolutely plastered.

"Oh didn't I tell you what happens?" she said. "They keep a supply of mattresses in those cupboards and we all kip down on the floor until we sober up."

*

I broke a big shire horse to harness for a London lady who had a boyfriend living in Chagford. She had bought the horse to save him from slaughter. When I finished breaking him it became obvious to me that she hadn't a clue about what to do with him. Up to this time knowledgeable people had owned all the horses that I had broken. Now I found myself having to teach someone from scratch all about working and caring for a horse.

A few years earlier I had bought a Welsh cob in Abergavenny market. She was one of the horses that I brought down from Cheltenham. I had made one bid for her, but the bidding went on far beyond what I could afford. I stopped paying attention, but the auctioneer suddenly asked me if I would stand to my one bid. I said I would; she was mine and she was known from then on as Just One. She was already broken to harness when I bought her.

In my youth I had heard tales of horse-drawn charabancs going out over the moor. They all finished in the late 1920s, but the idea of people paying for a carriage ride over the moor appealed to me.

I met a gypsy who told me he had a little Swedish waggonette for sale. I bought it and used Just One to drive the carriage about locally until she was well settled to it.

The big day came when I tested out the idea. I invited Mr and Mrs Geering, who were neighbours, to see if we could drive to Postbridge for lunch at *The East Dart Hotel*. The weather was kind to us. All went well. Just One made light of the hills. The next thing was to try to turn this idea into money. Never so easy as having the initial idea. I'd not heard of anyone doing this since the 1920s, so I had no model to copy. But it was proving to be a long hot dry summer – just the job for our new venture.

I approached a hotel in Chagford that had some American visitors. The trips proved to be popular and Just One and I worked as hard as we could. We were off to a good start.

At that time in Devon the Western Counties Heavy Horse Society had just been formed. There seemed to be some interest in working horses on the land. I, of course, had done a lot of this as a child. It was suggested to me that an advert in *Horse and Hound* might do some good. So I put an advert in for a

126

'Working Horse Weekend' and, low and behold, three people turned up.

I was in a complete funk. I had never planned or taught anyone on an organised course. They all turned out to be very nice people. We had a good weekend, but then they all wanted to stay for more days. I hadn't even thought of that happening, but they all stayed on. Howard Garbett, who was one of those first three, now lives nearby and I still see quite often.

That first week we ploughed with horses, we cut down a tree and hauled it back home from the woods. Mr Loran, who was an expert on pulling timber, came and advised us on this. Of course we also did lots of driving, but probably not in the same detail that I am able to go into these days.

I was very excited: it seemed that perhaps I'd found the answer to staying home while making a living and caring for my children. As I have been doing it ever since, I wasn't so far wrong.

PART 2

Dartmoor Driving

CHAPTER 8

Dartmoor Driving underway – and hits problems

I quickly found that there was more interest in private driving than in working horses on land. At that time there were no qualifications to be had, but I felt that I could do with a bit of instruction myself, as indeed I still like to learn anything I can.

Frank and Cynthia Haydon, who are well-known world-class experts in driving and hackney horses, were running some driving courses up on the Cotswolds. I had sold a horse well, so I decided to put some of the money into a week's instruction. All went well. It gave me a lot more confidence, which I was sadly lacking after all the bad times. I learned about the Achenbach system of driving horses. More than one hundred years after its development by Von Achenbach it is still internationally recognised as the best system.

I had advertised Working Horse Weekends, but in conversation with a potential customer she had told me that she didn't want to work on horses all the weekend. I saw her point and so I changed the name to Harness Horse Weekends, which may have helped make clearer what we were doing.

*

Pairs

I had driven Pairs during my National Service days. I managed to buy some new army harness from a saddler in Newbury. Some of it, although it had never been used, was stamped 1916. I was not aware of foreign harness available at that time. This army harness was indestructible. The traces were wire hawsers covered in leather.

I was able to use the Swedish waggonette to start with, but the lack of hydraulic brakes on the steep hills around us was making life difficult. I have never been an engineer, so I couldn't build anything suitable myself.

I had found a man who had made me some two-wheeled exercise carts, so I asked him if he could make me up a waggonette using motor car wheels with hydraulic brakes. He duly made it – and what a difference having good brakes made. I am well aware that some people say that brakes are not traditional, but safety had to come first. I'd heard that people had tried hydraulic and disc brakes on wooden wheels with bad results. Using car wheels may not have looked so pretty, but I was able to make driving safer.

The new waggonette soon proved its worth. I found that I could safely go down hills that I would never have dared to take on before. It opened up some different routes.

I later started a trip to South Zeal going through Chagford to *Gidleigh Park Hotel*. I got permission to use an old drive that led up to Gidleigh itself and then on to Moortown Gate, right along beside the moor, to South Zeal where we used to stop at *The King's Head*. They had a paddock where we could let the horses have a roll and a graze before we harnessed up to go home. The landlord had served in Burma with pack mules. They always gave us a great reception.

We often used a pony called Nobby as a cockhorse on this route, as in, "Ride a cockhorse to Banbury Cross". People would take it in turn to ride him on in front and warn traffic we were coming or to open gates in the park, then we would hook him on in front to help us up the hills.

A local hotel rang me up to ask if I could take a group of young ladies on this trip. Well, of course I could. I arranged to pick them up from the hotel.

They were all very glamorous – real page three girls. The cockney gentleman who had booked the trip saw us off. We had a nice happy trip to South Zeal. When we got into the bar, the cockney gent was waiting to buy us all drinks. In fact the supply of drinks seemed endless. We had an even happier return trip. We had to make a stop for nature's demands, but then we went on our merry way. We'd gone a couple of miles before we realised that we were one short.

At that moment a young farmer came towards us in his

battered old Landrover, so I told him that we had lost a glamorous blonde and asked if he could rescue her. He was off like a lurcher after a rabbit. He found her and they became long time partners! It seemed we were a dating agency as well.

These girls came for several years while I was at Stinhall. I was also doing a route down the Teign valley to Fingle Bridge. This is a lovely trip down beside the river, most of it off-road along a forestry track. At the start of one of these trips the cockney gent said he would meet us at the pub with his roller. I had a vision of him driving a steamroller until it dawned on me that he meant his Rolls-Royce.

When I finally plucked up courage to ask him about all these glamour girls, he shrugged and said, "I'm in the porno business." Oh well, we've all got to make a living I suppose. They were all great fun and very generous.

Coming back up beside the river this steady pair of cobs stopped and refused to go any further. I hadn't a clue what was upsetting them. I remembered that the landlord of the pub had just told us that some anglers claimed to have seen The Grey Lady. She was the ghost of Sarah Whiddon who was shot on her wedding day in Chagford church by a jealous lover. I asked my girl groom, Tona Cruickshank, if she could see anything that was upsetting them. She got down and had a look, but she could see nothing. Suddenly I had a wild idea. Out loud I asked the ghost if she would move aside, as we wanted to go home. The cobs walked forward with no more bother. I never saw any ghost. But the horses had sensed something.

While I'm on the subject of ghosts, Jay's Grave is beside the road from Chagford to Ashburton on the route that the wool wagons used to use between these two towns. In the eighteenth century Kitty Jay was a servant girl who got pregnant as a result of receiving the attentions of the squire's son. When it became known that she was pregnant, the squire threw her out. She was an orphan from the Poor House and with no one to turn to she hanged herself in the barn. As she had committed suicide she couldn't be buried in the churchyard and her grave lies at the junction of the road and a farm track. Her grave always has flowers on it and the local legend is that nobody knows who places them there. I was driving a pair towards the spot and telling my American guests the story. Just as we got to the grave a car pulled up, a young girl jumped out, placed flowers on the grave, jumped back in and drove off. She made me look a bit silly.

An odd sequel to this story is that on the day that I am writing this I had to pass the grave on my way to collect a load of hay from a nearby farm. The farmer told me that there had been two recent sightings near the grave of a female ghost who appeared to have no legs. I had never before heard any account of such a ghost.

The Rolling Stones used to rent an isolated cottage, called Stannon, out in the middle of the moor. I took a party of them on a trip one Easter when it fell early in the year. I had some of them in the waggonette and others riding horses. It came on to snow. Some of the girls really weren't dressed for that kind of weather, so we hurried along. The ones riding horses caused me a lot of anxiety as they wouldn't stay close. I was worried in case they became separated in the snow or got stuck in a bog. I think I read that the same guys got into trouble with a boat not long afterwards.

I had a letter recently from a lady who is now doing driving competitions. Many years ago she came to us on a driving course. Her letter reminded me that when she left us she had to get to Newton Abbot to catch a train. She was very surprised when I told her that I would drive her there with the pair, as the station is nearly twenty miles away. As it happened, I'd promised to take the pair to give carriage rides at a country sports fair at Newton Abbot racecourse, so it worked out well.

*

Team

For many years I had dreamed of driving my own four-in-hand. There was nobody in the Westcountry who was driving one at that time. I applied to go on a course at a well-known establishment up country, but at the last moment they rang up to say they couldn't take me.

Back in the fifties I had ridden beside Mr Gilbey on his

coach in London. I had made a promise to myself that if it was ever possible I would have and drive my own coach. I now had two good steady pairs going to work, but I didn't know how to get them going as a four.

The only source of information I could find was Morley Knight's book on driving. It is written in Victorian language, which sometimes makes it difficult to understand. It also, of course, only writes about the coachman's style of driving.

I copied a rein machine from his book and tried to teach myself how to use it.

The great day arrived when I thought that I was ready to try out my technique. I got some help organised. As the lanes around Stinhall are very narrow, we thought it best if Liz rode her horse in front to stop any traffic in a place where we could pass. I had a rather elderly lady, Mrs Ensor, who had horse experience, hold the leaders while I got sorted out. I also had a young Swedish girl, Annie, who was helping us that summer.

Liz rode off as outrider, but the leaders tried to follow her and knocked Mrs Ensor over. She then said that she didn't want to come. Liz was out of earshot heading off to stop any traffic. I just had to go on. When I got out on a bigger road I asked the Swedish girl something. There was no reply. I looked over my shoulder and there was no sign of her. She had decided to stay and check that the old lady was all right.

Meanwhile, Liz was doing just what we had agreed she was to do. She was trotting on stopping the traffic, but I never got close enough to make her hear. So on we went. I was trying to remember what Morley Knight had written. If he was watching me from that road in heaven where all old coachmen go, he must have been having a good laugh. However, all went well and we made it safely home, even if the sweat was trickling down my back.

How quickly the best-laid plans of mice and men can go astray. I did a lot more practising on the rein machine after that, but having had a go there was no holding me.

From then on, Liz drove a car in front, which didn't upset my cobs and I managed to get some better help. By the end of the summer I was becoming much more confident and coping with the coachman's style of team driving.

By the following summer I was doing some long trips right up to Sheepwash in North Devon.

We would stop at Sue and Maurice Maude's farm, where the hosts laid on a great party, and then we drove home, stopping at a few pubs along the way.

I was on the committee of Chagford show when the next show was being discussed. I rather rashly said that I would put on a cowboy show, loosely based on the film *Calamity Jane*. So I was given the task of making it all work. Not so easy when you have to rely totally on everybody else doing their bit.

We could only manage one rehearsal and that was on the night before. I'd enlisted the help of the Pony Club as the U.S. cavalry and the Young Farmers as the Red Indians. I was driving the team. Margaret Mainwaring was playing Doris Day – in fact she was a really good lookalike. Her husband was the Indian Chief. Mrs Brian Froude, who is an American, provided lots of very smart girls all in correct American country dress to be the saloon girls.

The saloon was built on a farm trailer.

My daughter, Honor, was in charge of the Pony Club cavalry. There was a large oak tree in the middle of the old Chagford show ground. We arranged for a Young Farmer to leap from the tree and kidnap Calamity Jane as I cantered the team underneath. He missed us the first time around so we had to go around again. The cavalry charged the stockade of Indians. One of the Pony Club cavalry was carrying the flag. The old pony ran away and nearly wiped out the Indians.

A local publican had lent me a huge empty whisky bottle, which I had filled with cold tea, and was pretending to drink as we cantered around the ring, the whisky bottle in one hand and the reins of four horses in the other. We all came out of the ring to a great round of applause.

I had just pulled up when a local lady came up to me and told me that I should be ashamed of myself.

"Whatever would your mother and father have said to see you so drunk?" she shouted. I offered the bottle of cold tea, but she wouldn't believe me or try it. I was stone cold sober!

I took the team to Bicton, not to compete, but to provide publicity for a TV advertising shot for the trials. I was still a

136

long way from being able to compete with a team.

I was continuing all the while with the instruction. In those days there was hardly anybody providing instruction, but there was a tremendous interest in learning to drive. My early idea of teaching farm work with horses was not proving to be the main attraction. Almost everybody wanted private carriage driving. At first we did just weekends. I would have nearly every weekend through the summer booked up. This helped with the money, as I was by then getting into a bit of trouble with the bank, but I also had to buy more equipment to cope with demand.

As we got busier we began taking people through the week, as well as at weekends.

I was getting a lot of practice in teaching. As luck would have it I have been told that I am a natural teacher. I have met many people who are an expert in their field, but cannot teach it.

This is years ago now, but the funny thing about it is that I can remember a lot of those early customers quite clearly. A special one was the lovely Polish model who came with her highbred mother. Wow!

*

Training Horses

The business of teaching driving came about as a result of me breaking horses to drive. Over the years I have learned a lot of new ways to get horses going in harness, quickly and quietly.

The best change was the building and use of the round corral. I first found out about it through a cowboy book on breaking horses. This was over thirty years ago when all cowboy horsemanship was completely beyond the pale. I have often wondered why the round corral was never heard of in this country. I had been with horses for all of my life but I had never come across one in Britain.

I have built an oval trotting track, which is proving a great help as it means that I can drive horses around it without the help of a groom. In fact, because it keeps horses a bit shut in, they rarely go badly in it.

But this is not a book on how to train horses. I have always learned more when things have gone wrong: at the very least I learn not to try that again.

Horses getting too much food and not enough work, plus some of the owner's odd ideas, can cause a lot of trouble. Motor transport makes the life of modern horses much easier than when we had to ride miles to a meet of the hounds, hunt all day and then ride home in the dark.

It has always given me great satisfaction when I have managed to get a horse going well.

*

TV and film work

I don't know if it was the result of the advertising shots for Bicton, but a television director rang me to ask if I could provide horses and several other things, such as chickens in crates made of hazel sticks from the hedges. They wanted them for the filming of *The Onedin Line*.

"No problem," I said, but then I had to go out and cut the hazel and teach myself how to make the crates. They also wanted calves, barrels, old implements, and lots more. I jumped at the chance as I was always looking for ways to earn some cash.

We took everything they wanted, plus any extra stuff that I could find, to Exeter Docks in our old Austin lorry. We were there for several days. It was fascinating, but the endless waiting about was hard to cope with.

I heard that they were moving on to film in Dartmouth and were having trouble finding enough horses to pull carts. I volunteered to provide three.

We duly arrived there with a young shire horse that I had just broken to harness, an old Dales mare who was a good harness horse and another cob who knew his job.

This part of the series was set in the time when ship owners were trying to change to steam-powered ships. Our main job was to haul coal from the coal merchant's yard along the docks to the ships. We had to be made up by the make-up girls and dressed with big black sacks pulled on over our heads.

One of my helpers, who was a very handsome young

farmer, disappeared into the make-up girls' caravan for a long time and we ragged him a bit about this.

I drove the shire horse myself as I was more than a bit worried that he might find it all more than he could cope with. As it turned out, he was as good as gold.

The film people asked me to provide a calf that they wanted to load onto the sailing ship by hoisting it aboard with a derrick crane. This meant that I had to persuade a saddler to make a special harness for the job. I took over several pieces of army harness and between us we created something that looked as if it should do the job. Thank goodness, it worked perfectly on the day. I had to play the part of the cattle drover, so I had to be made up for it. The make-up girl did such a good job that when I climbed back into our lorry, Liz, who was sitting in the passenger seat, shouted at me to get out as her husband was coming back at any minute.

On another occasion I provided and drove a horse and tipcart for the film *Fight Against Slavery* in a sequence that was also shot in Exeter Docks.

I was later asked to provide a flat four-wheeled wagon for a film that was being made on the coast. Bill Oddie was starring in it. This wagon was to be pulled by a pantomime horse along the beach, with Bill driving it. However, the iron wheels just sank into the sand and it was going to be impossible for the pantomime horse to move it.

A clever man on the film crew suggested that they covered a concrete ramp that went down to the sea with sand to make it look like the beach. Then they attached an almost invisible wire to the back of the wagon so they could let it gently run down the ramp. After it was filmed they could make it look as if the panto horse was pulling it along the beach.

Finally, all was ready. Off they went down the ramp. Bill picked up a big whip and pretended to whack the panto horse. To everyone's surprise an old lady rushed out of the crowd telling Bill not to be so cruel to the horse. We all collapsed in laughter, especially when a voice from the horse said, "That's right missus, you report him."

A version of *The Hound of the Baskervilles* was being filmed near Hound Tor. The film people made a lot of alterations to Mr Whitley's farm. Some of the plastic granite was so realistic that it was hard to believe it wasn't rock. I played the part of a farrier which, as a registered farrier, wasn't too difficult. I had to provide a horse, the forge and tools. I never got to see the film, so I don't know if my performance made it through the editing.

Years later when Maggie and I were together, I was asked to drive a team of horses for the block-buster film, *Out of Africa*. At £100 a day it was too good an opportunity to miss, even though I was hardly well enough after suffering a heart attack to do that sort of work. It was filmed in the winter in East Anglia, and was exceptionally cold. Waiting around all day did nothing to help me keep warm. The film crews sprayed everything with lime to make it look like snow, but after a couple of days work, it did snow overnight. This meant that the continuity was all wrong and the filming had to be started again. I just kept thinking of the extra money! After the film was released, Maggie and I settled down one evening to watch my "performance". We were just part of a long line of carriages in the opening scene, and were so far away that we could scarcely tell if I was driving a pair or a team!

I liked the extra money from film work, even if it wasn't the goldmine that some seem to think, but I really wasn't too keen on the endless waiting about.

*

Competition driving

I had seen Christine Dick scurry driving at the Devon County Show and thought it looked really good fun. I had taken photos of some of the carts and I found an engineer who was willing to have a go at making one.

I had broken two wild Dartmoor ponies to go in the cart. I called them Hootsie and Tootsie. Tootsie never made a good harness pony, but I managed to borrow another pony, called Thuggy, from Jean Alexander. Although they were still a bit wild they certainly went like the clappers. I did manage to get to a few shows, but I think that the best I did was at an indoor show in the middle of Bodmin Moor. Mr Robertson, the boss of the Trago Mills discount stores, had built a huge indoor stadium and organised a big pre-Horse of the Year Show event there.

The ponies had never competed anywhere before, let alone in an inside arena, and they were really frightened by all the noise. They more or less ran away, but I managed to miss all the cones and did one of the fastest rounds of the day.

We were all thrilled to bits.

Apart from the Devon County Show, I believe that all the scurry classes were up country at that time, so were really beyond the reach of our old transport. The lack of money and transport didn't help. I never felt that I should be enjoying myself at the shows when I might have been earning money.

Liz and I took a horse to compete at a little show at Tipton St John in East Devon. This show class was one of the first (if not the first) to run a class that had cross-country and cone driving all in the same class.

Roy Stewart, an old friend of mine, was also in this class. We had a bit of good-natured ragging each other to the delight of the spectators. I think we won one year and he won the next.

The man running this little show was the main organiser when it was decided to run the first ever Bicton National Driving Trials. Not long before the big day, he rang me to ask if I would enter a horse in The Grouse Novice Class as they were short of entries. I agreed to take Barney, a hairy little cob with a great heart, even though I had never even seen such an event. I had just taken delivery of the first ever Fenland Gig to be built. I only got it the night before the competition, so had never even used it. I had such a lot of fun that day driving across Woodbury Common. To my surprise I won and the organiser asked me how I felt about going to Windsor.

"Why do you ask that?" I said, quite unaware that I had just qualified for the Grouse Final at Windsor. I wasn't at all ready to take part in such an important competition. On the other hand I realised that it was most unlikely that I would ever get the chance again.

So off we went with Barney again in our old Bedford lorry and duly arrived at Windsor. I don't think I had ever seen so many ultra-smart horseboxes. We had a super time. We were told that we'd won and were awarded the prize. Then they told

141

me that we'd lost it in a recount. I still maintain I was first past the post. That's just the way the cookie crumbles, as they say. The Duke of Edinburgh invited us to a party one evening. A great honour, I felt. On the way back from the party a little girl was standing in the middle of the road in a wooded part of the park, waving wildly. I stopped and asked her what was wrong. She told me that her daddy had fallen in a ditch down in the wood. I ran down to the ditch as fast as I could. Sure enough, he was in up to his head with his wife holding his head above the water. We got him out, back to his lorry and back home. After all these years, I had a phone call from his wife only the other night.

*

The business had really begun to take off. The driving was becoming much more successful and the trekking bookings were going up every year. The trouble was that I had run up such a huge overdraft that it was proving impossible to earn enough money to reduce it. It was a constant source of great worry to me. I really can't handle money worries and my relationship with Liz was suffering.

A friend suggested that if I could get planning permission to convert a derelict barn, I could sell the farmhouse for twice what it would cost to convert the barn. If this plan worked as hoped for, it meant that I could have a purpose-built house and be able to take B& B customers. I would also be able to clear my overdraft.

I managed to get outline planning permission and foolishly thought that was the green light to get busy.

I sold the old house to Brian Froude and his wife, which gave me the money to pay for the conversion. I bought two caravans to move into while we did the work and started on the project. I hadn't realised that The Dartmoor National Park Authority were about to put forward every objection that they could possibly think of in order to obstruct any progress. They managed to delay us for some two years. During this time the price of building materials rose steeply and the amount of work involved increased. This meant that all my sums were going wrong.

142

I was unlucky enough to start with a well-recommended builder who proved to be a complete cowboy. I chased him off the site with a shovel!

All work was at a standstill, so I went to *The Ring of Bells* pub to console myself. A man hurried into the pub to announce that the old and well-established building firm of Stone's had gone broke and that all their men had been laid off. I could hardly believe my ears. Their manager had been to see me about doing my barn, but when he asked for fifty thousand pounds up front I had told him to get lost. So if I had agreed, my money would have gone down the drain. What a lucky escape I had had.

I quickly downed my drink and went to Stone's yard. I saw Alan Rice, who everybody knew was one of Stone's best stonemasons, standing with a group of other workers. They all looked completely lost. Most of them had only ever worked for Stone's.

I offered Alan the chance to work for me and he jumped at it. I asked him to pick some of the other men who could help him. I was back in the business of converting the derelict barn.

Alan knew just how to tackle all the difficulties, so with his help and advice progress was made. It was by now wintertime and the weather was making things difficult. The barn had a tile roof that was worth a lot of money if we could get them down. The trouble was that the roof was only just staying up. It was going to cost a lot of money to hire scaffolding to prop up the roof in order that the men could take these tiles off. I had a lorry load of straw booked, so when that arrived I stacked it tight to the roof so that we could work safely to take the tiles off. Most of the front wall had fallen out so we had to clear all the stones away in order to make a start rebuilding it. The building inspector insisted that we dug out a lot of natural granite that would have been in the foundations of the new wall. So we had to do this, even though Alan thought this was unnecessary and a waste of money. Nevertheless, we had to hire a pneumatic drill to move this stone.

At one stage we were stuck with a large boulder blocking our way. We couldn't reach it with the digger to move it, so I suggested that if I hooked our cob Barney to it with some chains he might be able to move it. I duly hooked him to it and the men helped with crowbars. Barney tried it once, but failed to shift it. He then gave an enormous lunge forward. He pulled the rock up onto a bank and stopped. I suddenly realised that Alan's car, that was his pride and joy, was right in the way. Barney gave another terrific leap forward and the rock was air-borne! The rock just missed the car.

The National Park insisted that we build a stone face to the barn. We were short of suitable granite, but I had a field bank that was made of some good quality stone. I hauled this up to the barn with Barney, using a sledge just as the farmers used to do years ago.

I felled some oak trees from my wood down in the Coombe and dragged them up to the house with the horses. These were to become the main beams in the house.

The weather came in very cold. We were really freezing in the caravans and I got Alan to complete a lean-to that was going to be the kitchen. We fitted a great big woodburner and made up our beds on the floor. We had a party one night and most of us just went to sleep on the floor. Alan was a bit shocked when he woke us all up in the morning!

I was still running the business while managing the conversion. In the end, all the work and worry proved too much for me. I was working a new pony one morning when I got some terrific pains in my chest. I managed to tie the pony up and rang my doctor. Fortunately, he was there and drove straight to see me. He found that I was having a heart attack. He rang for an ambulance and rode in it with me to Exeter Hospital. He later told me that he didn't think that I would make the hospital.

When the doctors were working on me soon after I arrived one said to the other one that I might just survive as I had never smoked. I don't think that I was meant to hear this, but I did and I announced that, "I was going to bloody survive."

I was in intensive care for about a week. When I was allowed to go into a general ward, the doctors came around doing their daily inspections. To the surprise of both of us, one of these doctors was the father of a girl called Tona, who had worked for me as a groom. He stopped and had a chat with me. After that I always seemed to get more attention from the nurses

33 Out hunting on Isca with Rose Gaisford on Solo, winter 1996.

34 Tandem of Mr Allen & Badger at Michelcombe, 1998.

35 Ponies in the Knapp.

36 Junus.

37 Junus, who started our line of Morgans,
showing the distinctive head.

38 Driving Mr Allen to a King's carriage, summer 2000.

39 Six-in-hand to Postbridge, September 2001.

40 A very steep turn onto the old A38; coach drive to Bridestowe, May 2002.

41 Lee 'driving' Pip & Scammel, summer 2003.

42 Driving John Parker's Norwich Mail Coach, summer 2004.

43 Driving Victoria & Mr Allen at Scorriton Flower Show.

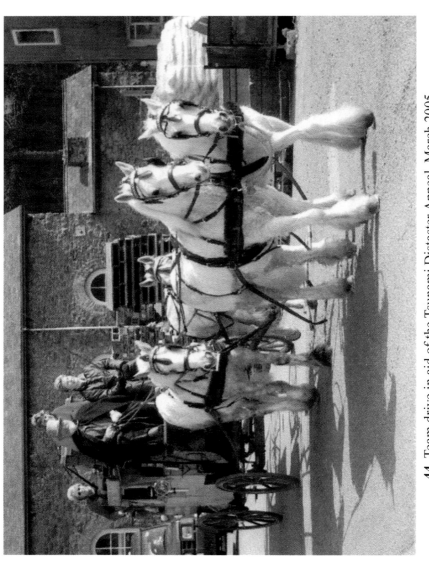

44 Team drive in aid of the Tsunami Distaster Appeal, March 2005.

45 Relaxing with Carolyn Owen at Michelcombe.

46 Padgent returning home after a lesson.

47 With Lee and Carolyn as groom, Padgent & Victoria
in the wheel, Badger & Dusty as leaders, May 2006.

48 Victoria & Padgent, Nicki Gaisford as groom, July 2006.

than the other patients. Perhaps it really does help to have friends in high places.

Eventually I was discharged. I still had all the money troubles and I had to try to go back to work, but I was much too weak to cope with it. I struggled on as best as I could, trying not to let customers see how ill I was. I also realised that my marriage to Liz finally was on the rocks.

I became suicidal with all these troubles and decided to end it all. I had a bottle of whisky and a bottle of sleeping pills. I was sitting in the new kitchen and was looking at the pills when the phone rang. The call was from an old friend who said that she had been having terrible feelings that something was badly wrong with me. So I told her what I was about to do. She told me in no uncertain terms not to be such a bloody fool and to chuck the pills into the fire. I did as I was told, but I drank the bottle of whisky.

Liz wanted a divorce. I could see that this was the only way out of the mess. Everything had to be sold to find the money to pay Liz, to get rid of my overdraft and, hopefully, to pay all the outstanding bills.

I was so ill that I felt that none of it really mattered any more as I was probably going to die any way.

I still had Barney and my competition gig and as I was now in open class F.E.I. competitions I thought that I might as well compete for what I thought would be my last season on earth. To hell with the money and responsibilities, I thought. I wasn't going to be around to sort out the mess anyway. I think that I did four national competitions that year. I was thrilled to collect third place at Sandringham in the Open. I went all the way to Lowther Park in Cumberland, but this was a dismal failure. I also competed at another event that was held where *To The Manor Born* series was filmed. It just rained for all three days – and my ancient Bedford leaked like a sieve. I also competed at Bicton, but I can't remember much about that one – except that I know that I got very drunk one night!

In the event, I survived. Death didn't save me from having to face up to reality.

Liz moved out.

I still had people booked on one last course. I certainly

145

didn't realise that this course was to change the rest of my life. There were four people booked on it. Two were a married couple; one was a young girl from North Devon and the other one was Maggie.

I was very suspicious of her. A lady reporter in the horsey press had been going around trekking stables and writing up reports. They may well have been accurate, but she certainly pulled no punches in her articles. I had warned my grooms about this lady, and we were all being very careful to keep everything up to scratch. I thought that Maggie might be her, but I couldn't find out for sure. Not that it would really have mattered in the circumstances.

Just after I managed to run that course, the barn conversion was sold.

I rented a cottage on a winter let from some friends and Clare and I moved in. Honor was away at college.

I had a small amount of capital left from Stinhall, but we would soon have nowhere to live and I wasn't well enough to work.

CHAPTER 9

Moving to Michelcombe

The French family had owned Michelcombe from before the war. It had been part of the Holne estate. John French was selling off the valley in a number of separate lots. A bit of luck for me was that for some reason he had been having difficulty selling a recent barn conversion, which we later called The Brookings. I went down to see him about buying it.

I didn't have an appointment, but just took a chance that he would be around. When I arrived I immediately loved the look of the place. I knocked on the door, but there was no answer so I started to look for John in the yard. I had bought some hay from him the year before, so I knew him slightly, He was nowhere around, but suddenly an old man shouted at me from over the next door hedge.

"Who the hell be you? Us don't want any bloody furriners about yur!" This was all in broad Devon dialect.

"I'm no bloody furriner," I replied. "I'm a Dartmoor man same as you and I've come to buy this place off John. Do you know where the hell he be?"

"Oh well, that's different. I think that he's up the Gibby Coombe."

"Where be that to?" I asked, and he directed me up the track. I found that this man was called Henry and he was John's uncle. I met John and we were able to quickly shake hands on the deal. I had just enough money left to be able to pay for it, without getting a mortgage or having to have a survey. Having shaken hands on the deal I considered the house and land to be mine, but of course I knew that I would have to wait for the solicitors to get themselves into gear.

This turned out to be the best deal that I have ever done.

Maggie rang up to book another driving course. On the

147

previous course I hadn't talked to the clients about my problems, so now I had to explain the situation to her. I'd had to sell most of the horses, but I still just about had what I needed in the stables at Stinhall.

Maggie came for a course and stayed with us in the cottage. She stayed for a few days, but on one of them it poured with rain. I said we could still drive if she wanted to, but she agreed that it wouldn't be very pleasant. I offered to take her to Michelcombe to show her the property I was buying. Not for a moment did either of us think that this was to be our future home.

We met John French and his partner, Carol, and they showed us around. They were moving next door and they showed us that as well. Rainwater was pouring off the road, through the front door of what was going to be their kitchen, and out of the back door. There was no ceiling and we could see right up to the corrugated asbestos roof.

I don't think that Maggie had ever seen anything like it.

As I had to be out of the holiday cottage in time for Easter, I was pushing John for possession.

He said, "You can't expect Carol (who had just had a baby) to move into a house in this state." I replied that Carol could stay, but he would have to go next door! He didn't think much of that idea.

Clare and I eventually moved into The Brookings. I thought that I'd paid Liz all that I had to; I'd paid for the house and cleared all my debts. I was feeling a bit better about things. But the yard was high in weeds; there was a Dutch barn, but no stabling and I'd had to sell the lorry and a lot of equipment. I needed to earn a living, but I had no idea how I was going to do it. After the heart attack I had been left with angina that was so bad that I could scarcely walk across a room.

Clare was by then a teenager with all a teenager's problems, but they had been made much worse by the upheaval the poor girl had suffered. She was helping out at Frost's racing stables at the weekends and evenings.

I thought that as I'd been self-employed I couldn't claim any State benefits. Nobody had told me about disability benefit, until my doctor mentioned it to me. I could have been claiming it ever since the heart attack. When the payments started, it certainly helped. I was very willing to work, but I really wasn't capable of doing so full time – if at all.

My friend, Howard Garbett, came back to Devon from doing his saddler's course at Cordwainers in London. While he found somewhere to live, I offered him the use of an old caravan that had come with the property. One of his friends came to visit him. They had both been mercenaries in the Congo. There was something really intimidating about the friend.

The divorce still wasn't sorted out. I was receiving a stream of nasty letters from Liz's solicitors. The three of us were sitting at the kitchen table one morning when I opened one of the letters. They could see that I was upset, so I explained to Howard and his friend what was going on.

Later that morning I was driving them through Chagford, when I happened to see the solicitor walking past *The Three Crowns*.

I said, "There's the bastard that keeps writing those letters."

Howard's friend produced a big revolver from a pocket. He said, "I'll take the bastard out before he reaches the other side of the village square." Then he went on to tell me to park the car near the square and leave the keys in the ignition so that he could take the car afterwards. And he told me to go into the pub and make sure that people knew I was there.

There was absolutely no doubt in my mind that this man was quite capable of doing it. I was appalled. Apart from any other considerations, I had enough problems without being mixed up in murder. It was really difficult to talk him out of it. It was a shock to learn that such people existed.

Sometime later this mercenary was found dead in suspicious circumstances in Southampton. Many years later I had to see this same solicitor about another matter. I told him that he owed his life to me. He just laughed. He didn't think that I could be telling the truth.

I still had some horses left at Stinhall, but I was too ill to think of riding them back to Michelcombe. I couldn't afford to hire a lorry, but I was saved by Debbie Ogle, whom I had helped a little with her carriage driving. She kindly offered to take me in her father's lorry to collect them. It was the last time I was in Stinhall yard.

I went and saw my old friend Sam Harris, who was the well-known Dartmoor scrapman, to ask him if he had any sheets of galvanised iron that I could use to make stables. Sam turned up trumps as he had just bought a shed on a farm for scrap. He offered to get his men to take the shed down, deliver it to me and put it back up. He knew my money problems and he just told me to pay him when I could. When I looked reluctant he told me not to worry as he could always take the shed back. I did indeed pay him later. He really was such a good man.

Sam got terribly burned trying to burn out a scrap car, but refused to go to hospital. His wife treated him with herbal remedies. I visited him in his old caravan while he was ill. I had a friend with me who had worked as a nurse at Frenchay burns unit and she told me that Sam hadn't any chance of getting better – but he did.

I was having great difficulty getting enough money together to buy the weekly groceries. I bought a bag of potatoes and I had some chickens. We lived on egg and chips for most of the time.

I used to drive my Dartmoor pony to Buckfastleigh to buy whatever other supplies I might be able to find some cash for. I certainly couldn't afford to drive the car down there. I used to tie the pony to a lamppost while I did what shopping I could.

I couldn't afford to buy wood, so I cut down an orchard with my chainsaw to get enough wood for the fire to get us through the winter.

I very sadly realised that the only way I could raise some money was by selling two of my old horses. They were too old to be sold for anything other than slaughter. It was an awful decision, but I was running out of hay for them.

About the only good thing that winter was my growing friendship with Maggie, who was providing a lot of moral support from London. We were getting on well, although we were from very different worlds. She was single and had worked for British Telecom for a long time. I braved taking the bus to London to see her.

The secretary of The South Brent Riding Club rang me up

to ask if I would give a talk on driving to club members. I agreed to do this. Little did I realise that it was to be the start of things getting better.

It was pouring with rain on the day of my talk and only a few people turned up. I failed to get any feedback from them. I didn't feel that it had gone down at all well. I was really disappointed.

But strangely enough, Steph and John, who had attended the talk, brought me two liveries and I helped them to get their cob, called Morgan, going in harness.

Gilly Hawes, who also came that morning, introduced me to Bob and Shirley McKennee from New England who wanted to drive a four-in-hand of ponies and who became regular customers for fourteen years. The McKennees always came in the autumn and often had poor weather, but Shirley was never put off, despite her advancing years and the fact that she only had one leg. I heard recently that she had lost the other leg, but was still determined to go on driving the ponies that we had sent her. Sadly she died soon after this.

By this time my four ponies were all I had left from the wreckage. I was still having thoughts about competing with a team in the coming summer. I must have been completely nuts even to be thinking of such a thing. The ponies were still quite wild. I had no team harness, no competition cart, no lorry and no money to pay anybody to help. But I can be a bloody-minded old sod when I feel like it.

A hippy couple turned up who wanted to drive a horse-drawn carriage to New Zealand where her father was a sheep farmer. I thought that they were mad to have such an idea, but they wanted somewhere to pitch their tent, so I said that as long as they helped me get the pony team going, they were welcome to stay. This meant that I could start work with the team and the couple could learn about carriage driving.

There were yet more potential problems with the divorce, which didn't help at all. Divorce solicitors don't seem to think they are doing their job unless they manage to completely destroy the other side.

Honor finished her business studies course. I got a room ready for her. I was clinging to the idea that with her help I could get the business going again on a sound footing. But she told me she wasn't coming home, but was going to live with Paddy Gallagher – an Irish builder, who was a hard worker, but with the reputation for being a trouble-maker. I had no idea that they'd been seeing each other. It wasn't what I wanted to hear.

I was still having trouble with angina and I had difficulty working for more than half a day. I still had the idea that I was likely to die at any moment, so I suppose this in a way made me carry on regardless.

I decided to borrow some money secured against the house to finance this crazy idea of competing. I had almost no customers which meant I had time to work on the ponies. I remember that I rang Maggie to tell her that I had managed to drive the ponies around the oak tree at Gallant le Bower only weeks before I was hoping to compete with them.

I saw an advert for a Bedford T.K. lorry up in North Devon and I bought it.

I went to Reading Carriage Sales and managed to buy a very nice pony pairs set of harness. Howard was working to make up a set of team harness.

I met a dealer at Reading who told me that Bryan Wicks, who lived near Tetbury, had a Victorian pony waggonette for sale. When I arrived at his place I could see that it was in very poor shape, needing four new wheels. However I managed to do a deal and brought it home.

I found out that the lorry engine wasn't any good and I knew I'd have to have it changed.

I had entered the team for the Brighton Trials, but I could see that I couldn't possibly get ready to compete in time. I arranged to take Maggie there to show her what it was all about. As we walked past the competitors several of them, who had been on courses with me at Stinhall, came up for a chat. They all told me that they wouldn't have been there without my help. This greatly encouraged me to try and keep going.

I went home determined to go on with the team. I had entered trials at Osberton, near Nottingham.

I had another engine fitted in the lorry, but as they only fitted it the day before we had to leave for Osberton, it was untried.

My waggonette wasn't ready, but I managed to borrow a cross-country cart from a friend. Somehow I made room for everything in the lorry. Maggie had come down from London to help. The lorry never missed a beat all the way there and back. The ponies went as well as I could possibly hope for. To our great joy we completed the course successfully. It was a very encouraging start to our season.

We then took the ponies to our local national event at Bicton. We had some problems in the water, but otherwise managed to complete the course successfully. I managed to finish in third place, so I was well pleased.

We were still using the borrowed vehicle which was a proper battle waggon, made for the job, but when the husband of the lady who was lending it to us saw how fast we had to drive it he blew a fuse and refused to let us borrow it again.

This meant that I had to get the old waggonette that I had bought on the road as quickly as possible. I found four steel wheels and got some brake fittings from the scrap yard. I found a firm that was prepared to put it all together, but once again we didn't have time to try it out before we went to Wyle in Somerset.

This was the last event of the summer. The money I had borrowed was nearly gone. I was determined to have one last go.

We had a truly wonderful day's driving. The waggonette drove like a dream. We had an elderly lady judge who rode with us. She was a real sport. We didn't have any troubles in the water this time and to my great joy I was second in the cone driving. I finished about fifth out of some twelve teams with some well-known names behind me.

Once again I had run out of money. I couldn't even afford to put enough petrol in the lorry to get home. I planned to drive the lorry until it ran out of petrol, then take the ponies out and drive them home on the road. Maggie insisted on lending me enough cash to get us home.

I was over the moon with my success. It was back to reality the next day, but I had some good news – Liz had told her solicitors to leave me alone.

I managed to get two horses to break to drive that winter. I had to fetch them from London and I went with the lorry to collect them. On the way back I ran into a heavy snowstorm on Salisbury Plain. I was lucky to make it back.

I was beginning to get more instruction as well, but the winter turned bitterly cold with more snow than I have ever seen since. The stable conversion was not the warmest place to be.

Maggie had been trying to get a transfer from her job with B.T. in Wimbledon to Exeter. She finally got the posting and she came to live with me. This was tremendous giving me a new lease of life. I knew that I just had to knuckle down to build up *Dartmoor Driving* into something special.

I decided to give up serious competitive driving as it was costing the earth.

I did, however, do one more event in France the following summer.

*

I have realised that although I've been talking about my pony team, I haven't told you anything about this little team of Dartmoors.

I had bought Bungle and Dodger at the old Chagford pony market when they were just wild foals. As they were both big strong colts I had to pay top price of the sale for them. This would have been about fifty pounds at that time. A lot of the ponies at the sale were sold for meat and meat prices were quite high then.

I bought the character of the team, called Woolley, privately from a local lady, who was a thalidomide victim. He was on the small side, but as he was very young I thought he might grow on. He didn't, but he made a super leader and has given us all such fun. He's not very sound now, but has a lovely retirement home with Rosemary Seel near Ashburton.

Gubbins was the only pure bred pony in the team. I bought him from a lady in North Devon to complete the team. He was being kept in disgraceful conditions, running with cattle in a yard practically up to his belly in deep slurry. I liked the look of him and also took pity on him. After I had paid for him in pound notes, the owner told me that she would come and inspect my place to make sure that he was being properly looked after! I just lost my rag and told her exactly what I thought of her ideas of looking after ponies. Why are there so many of these awful, stuck-up, and downright dangerous women mixed up in the horsey world?

I can't remember the name he had, but I called him Gubbins. There used to be a band of rogues living on north Dartmoor called Gubbins, just like the Doones on Exmoor.

Bungle and Dodger were wild ponies when I bought them, so I had to halter-break them, and handle them as much as possible. Dodger was always a bit jumpy, but Bungle became a very quiet, sensible pony, becoming the mainstay of my stables at Michelcombe, as far as instruction was concerned.

I was driving Dodger home through Scorriton one day when two farm collies attacked him. He leapt away from them, but the cart hit the wall and tipped me out. He galloped off down the road. The cart made him hit the parapet of the stone bridge, but he galloped on home.

I found him back in the yard with a terribly damaged knee. I got the vet out who quite sensibly told me to have him put down. I was very reluctant, so he gave me painkillers for the pony while I thought about it.

I decided to try and save Dodger. I fixed up a cold hose to pour water on his leg. I kept this up for days on end. I remembered that years before, Mother had cured Ruddy Pip's knee by putting Conucresin all over it, so I tried it. Then I smothered the knee in Stockholm Tar and turned him away on Dartmoor for some twelve months. I kept an eye on him. He came back healed up and sound. He is now with Tony & Christine Carden, in the South Hams, living a luxury retirement, along with his friend and work mate, Pip.

Looking back on those times I often wonder what on earth made me so determined to keep on trying to get this team going. Sheer bloody-mindedness perhaps!

*

I mentioned Henry French at the start of this chapter and this seems like the right time to say a bit more about him.

Henry was a real character. He had lived all his life in Michelcombe, working on the family farm.

One year, just before Christmas, he came to me saying that his two nephews wouldn't take him to the village shop and that he had no food in the house. I didn't believe him, but I took him to the shop. He bought a packet of Polo mints. I got a bit mad and told Garth, who ran the shop, to fill a big box with food that Henry would buy or I was going to leave Henry to walk home.

One day I was chatting to him by a farm gate when a walker came by. Henry asked him if he had a cigarette to spare. The walker produced a packet, opened it and held it out to Henry, who said, "Oh, I see you've got plenty," and took a lot more than one.

Henry came into our house one day wanting to telephone the doctor. Henry's personal hygiene left a bit to be desired. As luck would have it I had a phone with a long flex, so I put the phone in the porch. We heard him tell the doctor that he was very ill and needed him to come quickly. When Henry got back to the lane he met somebody he knew and stopped to talk to them. He was still talking when the doctor drove up in his car. We heard the doctor's voice quite clearly. I was a bit surprised at his language!

During the time that Howard Garbett was living in a caravan behind the stables, he came home late one night to find a Dartmoor colt that I had bought at Chagford earlier that day trotting up and down beside a fence and whinnying at a big carthorse that was trotting up and down the other side of the fence. He managed to catch the colt, but when he went back he couldn't find any trace of the carthorse. He was telling me this at breakfast the next day. I told him that I didn't have a carthorse on the place. At that moment Henry walked in and asked how the carthorse was marked. From Howard's description he instantly recognised his old horse, Briton, who was buried in that field.

Howard and I were struggling to clear an old barn of dried dung. It was at least two or three feet deep. We finally finished and went indoors to celebrate our achievement. There was an awful crashing sound from outside. We rushed out to the barn to find that a huge section of stone wall had fallen down. Henry's two walking sticks poked out of the rubble and we both thought that Henry was buried under it. We were frantically moving the stones when a voice from behind us asked what all the noise was about. Henry was standing there chuckling at us. He came very close to having a rock chucked at him.

Several times since his death both Maggie and I have felt his presence in the stables, but we haven't seen anything. We both feel that he is very benign; as if he is just watching what's going on around his old farm.

CHAPTER 10

BDS tests; Cherbourg; coach & carriage building; building stables

In my early years at Stinhall I took part in a charity drive organised by the BDS. I took a pair of cobs called Whinney and Barney and my Swedish waggonette down to South Brent to join the start. The drive followed the old coaching road out of South Brent up the long hill. The cobs were well used to hills, so this didn't bother them. This is a lovely stretch of road, with little or no traffic, and lovely views of the countryside.

There were some ten single turnouts, but I was the only pair.

A band of helpers did a good job of collecting money for charity from the houses, shops, schools and pubs along the way. We went down through the centre of Buckfastleigh and on to Ashburton using the old A38.

Soon after I started teaching I asked our District Commissioner about taking a British Driving Society test. Looking back on it, it was obviously in the very early days of the tests, because he told me that he knew nothing about them, so I didn't pursue the matter any further at that time.

However, many years later, not long after I was getting the business going again at Michelcombe, the BDS brought out a new set of driving proficiency tests. If I was serious about developing *Dartmoor Driving* (and I was) it seemed sensible to pursue any certificate that showed that we knew what we were doing, so I wrote to the BDS enquiring about taking these new tests.

I had taught Mo Francis, who came from Wales, to drive a four-in-hand team. I knew that she was an examiner for the BDS tests so I rang her up to ask for her help. She agreed to conduct the stage one and two exams at our stables and I arranged for

159

four of us (me, Maggie and two grooms) to take the tests over a weekend.

The great day arrived. We all passed stage one, but when it came to stage two, Nicky Gaisford decided that she didn't want to do it and the other girl failed, but Maggie and I passed.

I then applied to take Stage Three with Caroline Dale-Leech at Darley Dale, Matlock in Derbyshire. At the Red House Stables & Carriage Museum Caroline and her husband have a fine collection of historic horse-drawn carriages and equipment. It's all beautifully maintained, but it isn't shut away in a museum just to be looked at, the carriages are regularly used on the roads.

It was a long way from home, so it meant two nights away. When I arrived there was a briefing in her harness room and there were a lot of people there. I didn't realise that there were only about six of us that were actually doing the test on the following day. I kept very quiet, as I didn't want to call attention to myself. The next day we were passed from one examiner to another. The test was all done on an oral basis. At first I was hanging back a bit because all of the other candidates were ladies. I woke up just in time to realise that if I wanted to pass I must forget about being polite, open my mouth and ride a winner. In fact, one of the examiners had to ask me to keep quiet in order to give the others a chance to answer! I had the bit between my teeth and told her that there was no chance of that – I was there to pass.

The only hands-on test was to put on a set of pair's harness and put to the pair. After we had done that the examiner said that we had all failed – "Except you, Mr Arden."

What a relief that was. I was then allowed to drive the candidates around the town.

I was so chuffed at passing, but there was still Stage Four. I asked Caroline if I could also take this at her place. She agreed and we made a date for later the same summer.

As Stage Four is about driving team, tandem, and coaching, I needed to do some homework. I could drive the team and tandem, but was rusty on the coaching side and wasn't able to use a proper team whip. In fact, I didn't even own such a whip and I had to go to Reading Carriage Sales to try to buy one. As usual, my funds were very low; I knew that I would have to be extremely lucky to get one at all.

I only had an old Post Office van that kept overheating, so it took me a long time to get there and I missed the first two whips. Nicky Gaisford and her daughter, Rose, came up with me. She saw a top hat in the saddler's that she fancied, but she couldn't afford it. I needed all my money in order to try to buy a whip.

I finally managed to buy an old team whip that was made by George Schomberg. After I'd got it I offered Nicky some cash to help her buy the hat, but when she went back to the shop she found that it had been sold.

The whip had the lash wrapped tightly around the stick. It didn't look like it had been used for many years. As the lash was so dry, I didn't like to try to undo it until I had dressed it to get it supple. I only had about two weeks to do this and learn how to use it properly.

The various books I looked at all had different descriptions of how the whip should be used, but I didn't have anybody to show me the correct way. Also, I had customers every day, so I had to get up very early in the morning in order to get in some practice before anybody was about.

I thought I had just about mastered it in time for the test.

I had called on my friend, Colin Henderson, for some expert advice on coaching to help me with that part of the test.

I certainly wasn't full of confidence on the day. First Caroline asked me to demonstrate the use of the whip from a mounting block. My guardian angel must have been looking after me, as it went as if I'd been doing it forever. I was then asked to drive her team of horses. She told me that she had deliberately put a lazy leader in on the offside so that I would have to use the whip from the box seat. Once again it worked perfectly. I just couldn't believe my luck.

I was really thrilled when Caroline told me that I had passed Stage Four. I was well over sixty when I took these exams. I hadn't been given the qualifications on grandfather's rights, as some had been, but by genuinely taking the tests.

*

161

I had given up competitive driving the previous year, but an English team of driving turnouts was going to Cherbourg to compete against the French and they lacked a four-in-hand team as the event clashed with Brighton Trials. As they knew that we were no longer competing in other trials, the organisers asked me if we could go to France. I had to explain that I would love to go, but that I hadn't got any money. Sponsorship was arranged with a French radio station. We were on our way.

Our lorry was off the road. I only had a Series I Landrover and a flat trailer that I had borrowed for the trip. My old friend, Liz Newbolt-Young of Shilston Rocks Stud, kindly offered to take my ponies in her horsebox, if I took the carts and hay on my flat trailer.

There were miles of paperwork and vets inspections to complete before we left Weymouth. I had never taken any ponies on a boat before, or indeed been to France. It was all a great adventure.

After we had been unloaded in Cherbourg we formed up in a convoy to go to the farm where we were to stay. All the other competitors had their horseboxes to sleep in, but we only had a flat trailer. B&B was out of the question, as we couldn't afford it.

A kindly French farmer let us have the use of his carthorse stables. We put the ponies in the stalls and slept in the alley way behind them. We had taken a Calor gas cooker, supplies of food and bedding so Maggie and I were quite comfortable. There was a hen that laid an egg every morning in a manger and each morning we presented the egg to the farmer. I saw him milking his cows by hand out in the field and I milked a cow for him. He was most surprised that I could do this. We didn't speak a word of each other's language, but it still made for good relations.

The competition was held in the grounds of a grand chateau that provided a lovely setting. Le Committee, the French organising people, asked us to take part in a publicity drive through Cherbourg. I gladly agreed, but I'm ashamed to say that several other English competitors refused to join in.

We had a really sporty drive right through the middle of Cherbourg, well escorted by gendarmes. It was all something rather new for us.

The next day was the cross-country day, which was what we had really come for. Just as in England, a judge rode with us, but this judge had lots of radio equipment with him. As I don't speak French I didn't know what he was saying. It was a very demanding course with lots of real challenges. As we were far out, well away from the crowds, I must admit my language left a bit to be desired. Maggie kept shouting something at me, but I was too busy concentrating to listen properly.

As we neared the finishing line, I ran a wheel into a ditch that I hadn't seen and the judge was shot off his seat along with his radio equipment. As we collected ourselves together Maggie said, "I've been trying to tell you that he isn't a judge, he's a French radio reporter doing a live broadcast!"

All I could do was hope that not many French listeners understood English swearing.

The cone driving took place next day in an arena with a proper grandstand that was packed with spectators. I had been down and walked the course while Maggie got the ponies ready. I went back to the farm, but just as all the teams were leaving to go down to the arena, the farmer came out and invited us in for a drink. As there was plenty of time, we tied the team up to some rails and trooped into his house. He plied me with homemade Calvados, something I had never drunk before. There were lots of different bottles on a shelf that ran around the kitchen and I think I sampled quite a few. Maggie was only offered coffee!

Suddenly the English chef d'équipe came into the kitchen. He was not best pleased. He was an army officer type and he ordered us out a bit sharpish, together with remarks that we had come to compete not to get plastered.

We still had to wait for a long time before it was our turn to go into the ring. I could tell that he was still annoyed with me and that just made me more determined to show him something. The ponies really rose to the occasion. They just flew round the course. We cantered most of the way, didn't touch any cones and did the fastest clear round of the day. The French crowd just loved it. They were all shouting, "Encore!"

We won a big cup – much to the disgust of our chef d'équipe.

A French mail coach was driven into the ring. Four big, broad carthorses pulled it. I asked if I might be permitted to drive it, but I was told that, as the government owned it, there was no chance of this being allowed.

I have no idea why there was a change of mind, but a little while later I was invited to drive this team in the main arena. As luck would have it they went very well for me – even though I couldn't command them in French. I managed to do some figure of eights and slalom down the middle of the ring, much to the delight of the French spectators. This was a huge outfit compared to my Dartmoor pony team and it provided an added bonus on a wonderful day.

That night there was a big party in a marquee. As we were celebrating a delivery lorry backed into the end of the marquee and just kept coming, knocking over tables and scattering guests. Luckily he didn't hurt anybody, but he did create panic.

The following morning, after we had thanked our hosts, we headed back to the ferry.

Once on the boat we were told that we were not allowed to bring any hay back into England. Nobody had warned us, so we had to throw all we had over the stern of the boat. Some of it blew back onto the decks and got the crew a bit excited! We left a long trail of hay floating away behind us.

When we arrived at Weymouth it was a bit late, the customs officers just looked at our little convoy and opened the gates and let us go. We hadn't gone far before my old Landrover decided it had had enough and, luckily for us, ground to a halt near a pub. We had to treat ourselves to B&B at the pub. A hot bath and a proper bed were very welcome.

The local garage fixed the Landrover in the morning and we made it home.

What an adventure it had been!

*

I can clearly remember trying to build a pony cart during the war when I was still a child. I have no idea why I was trying to do this as my parents were only interested in hunting and racing. I didn't get any help, so it never got finished.

Many years later, Sally and I managed to put together an exercise cart made from an old trailer.

After I had moved to Stinhall and started teaching driving, there was a real need to get some exercise carts made. I saw an advert from a man in Cornwall who was making car trailers. I went down to see him and he agreed to make an exercise cart from my plans. This cart proved to be a great success. I had several others made and sold them. I had been using a traditional waggonette that of course didn't have hydraulic brakes. The same man made a good job of building me the four-wheeler with motor car wheels and hydraulic brakes that I mentioned earlier.

Unfortunately, he then sold me a Morris pick-up that he claimed to have restored. On the way home the brakes failed. I had to ask a local garage to mend it. To my horror they told me that vehicle was completely unroadworthy despite the fact that I had bought it with a brand new MOT test certificate. I rang my man up and asked him to refund my money. To my surprise, he flatly refused to help in any way. That was the end of our joint cart building.

I was recommended to an old man who lived in an isolated cottage hidden away in the woods. He made quite a few carts for me. His work was good and I always had a fair deal from him, but we lost touch during my problem time at Stinhall.

After I moved to Michelcombe, I asked a farmer's son, who was doing some welding on the local farms, if he could help me out. He knew nothing about making carts, so I had to spend a lot of time teaching him. Between us we made some really nice carts, but it turned out that his ideas of doing business were not the same as mine, so we went our different ways.

A small local garage also built some good carts for me. We still use a waggonette that they built, but like lots of small garages, he has closed.

When you teach driving it means that you are bound to meet people who want a cart of their own but, as you can tell, having carts made to sell just hasn't worked out.

Over the years many customers have wanted to make their own carts and I have always let them take measurements and photos, but very few of them seem to have had any success.

I have tried to help customers to get started as cheaply as possible. That is not so easy, as some would-be makers read about the prices that top manufactures charge advertised in Carriage Driving Magazine and then expect to be able to charge the same, but they lack the experience and reputation of the top firms. They are also unable to provide a back up with spares. I cater for beginners, and the lower end of the market, so have no need or market for expensive carriages. Recently I have been able to get Polish and Chinese imports via a couple of dealers that I have known for years. These vehicles are very much cheaper than their English counterparts and are ideal for us and our customers.

We were being asked to do more weddings every year, but we didn't have a suitable vehicle, such as a landau, for the job. I made enquiries about buying one, but the older ones didn't come with hydraulic brakes and the new ones were too expensive: I just didn't think that we would get enough weddings to justify the cost.

I had taken a few small welding jobs to a young man called Dave Hannaford who had set up as a welder in Ashburton. I knew he was looking for work, so I asked him if we could turn a waggonette that I owned into a landau. He agreed, as long as I stayed in his workshop and show him just what I wanted as we went along. He would do the steelwork while I did the woodwork.

We worked well together and gradually a landau frame emerged at a price that I could afford. I clad his steel frame with plywood.

I was sitting having breakfast one morning, gazing at a coaching print that hangs on my wall, when I suddenly realised that if I had a coach frame that fitted over the top of the landau, I could use the same vehicle for both weddings and coaching.

So I went back to Dave with the idea. Once again he did the steelwork while I clad it in thin ply in order to keep the weight down.

Gradually the two-piece coach took shape. I bought some chain-lift pulleys to lift the top on and off.

Finally, the great day arrived for us to test-drive it as a coach. Mike Oborn, who had been helping me with the building, came as groom. We put the ponies to and went down around the Buckfastleigh playing fields. I was very nervous, but all went well. There were still a lot of improvements to make, but at least we had succeeded in getting it on the road.

Not only does this one carriage give us either a landau or a coach, but it strips right down to a flat bed that we have used for funerals!

*

Over the years I have had to make my own stables at the different places that I have owned. It never occurred to me that such work needed planning permission – until recently.

When I moved to Michelcombe there was only an asbestos Dutch barn and that had a cider press right in the middle of it. I didn't want this press, so John French removed it for me. This turned out to be a very difficult job as it had been very well concreted in place.

I have already described going to Sam Harris and his kindly putting up a metal shed that I used for the four Dartmoors.

Although at that stage I was feeling so very ill, I started to get some horses to break which meant that I needed more stabling. I built two boxes at the back of the Dutch barn. I couldn't afford any concrete floors, or any help, but I managed to scrounge some wood and galvanised iron from a demolition site. I owned a chain saw so I built these two stables with the help of the chain saw and some six-inch nails. As more business came I had to build four more boxes. I arranged them in two lines running off the barn. The ground between them rapidly turned into a bog and I had to quickly put a roof over this area. This had the effect of creating an American barn type of stabling and kept the centre alleyway much drier. Some years later Peter Dodd and I managed to dig it out by hand and concrete it over.

I still had nowhere to keep carts and equipment in the dry and I was very short of yard space. I decided to try and make a much bigger yard down in the old orchard. This had a separate entrance from the road. The first problem was to remove a bank and clear a level base. I asked several contractors to price the job and I soon realised that there was no way that I could possibly afford this project.

Once again my guardian angel gave me a hand. I mentioned before the hippy boy who turned up with his horse and his girlfriend. They lived in a tent on my land while I broke the horse to harness and taught them to drive so that they could go travelling. When he heard about my problem he told me that he knew how to drive a digger. It so happened that a local man who had a digger owed me a small favour and he let us borrow the digger to get the job done.

We soon had the bank moved and the site cleared, but we didn't have enough backfill to level it up. I was driving a pony through the village when I met a skip lorry, loaded with hardcore, and driven by a man that I knew. He readily agreed to tip the skip into my yard and then brought load after load of good hardcore that had the yard levelled at no cost to me. I then needed a shed for my carts and a Dutch barn to store hay and straw.

This was some time after Maggie had moved down to join me. The business was getting back onto its feet and I was able to afford to pay Peter Dodd to help me erect these buildings.

My neighbour, Richard Parsons, was having a new farmhouse built and we agreed that he would send any surplus gravel coming off his site down to me to surface the yard.

Maggie and I had decided to get married.

Without realising it Richard chose to send all of the gravel down to me on our wedding day. Maggie was changing into her wedding dress when the lorries turned up. I realised that the ponies were all running in fields that led into the yard. This meant that we had to move them in case anybody left a gate open and let them out. So there was Maggie running about in her wedding dress catching ponies. It could only happen to me. We did finally make it to the register office.

Many years later I decided to clear up a real mess of rick sheets and galvanised iron that was over a rick of straw. Peter and I put up a nice tidy Dutch barn with a new purpose built shed next door to it. As usual, I hadn't bothered about planning permission, thinking that, even if it was needed, nobody would worry about it as I'd tidied up a real mess and made the place look so much better. But we had a neighbour who reported me to the National Park. I had to get retrospective planning permission which wasted a lot of time and cost over a thousand pounds. Such is life.

However, we do now have a very useful set of buildings that are all paid for.

CHAPTER 11

Early trips; longer journeys and the new coach

These are just a few recollections of some trips that Maggie and I, and some of our helpers, made from Michelcombe in the first years of our being there.

I've mentioned the American McKennee couple before: they came every autumn for many years and I taught Shirley to drive a four-in-hand. She was one of life's characters. Handicapped by the loss of a leg, nothing would stop her and she loved going for long drives over the moor. They came in the autumn when the weather was often bad, but the ponies were really fit at the end of the season and we used to cover some long distances. Shirley liked a whisky or two: she was always most generous in the pub. It was lucky that we didn't get breathalysed on the way home. I remember driving to Chagford for lunch, coming back by way of Widecombe, where we ran into a severe thunderstorm. It was quite alarming, but it seemed to bother me more than the ponies.

For one of our early trips my girl groom failed to turn up. Very wrongly I agreed to take the team out without a groom. This meant I only had Shirley's husband, Bob, to help. He was not at all horsey and somewhat frail. He wasn't likely to be able to help much if things went wrong. I certainly wouldn't do it today.

Off we went across Holne Moor heading for Postbridge. As we went down past Jolly Lane Cottage at Huccaby, Paul Gaisford, an artist who had done some driving with me, was in the garden. I asked him if he would like to ride with us. He didn't want to come, but a smart young woman in a fancy straw hat who was with him said that she would love to come. This was a turn up for the books. I had lost one girl groom, but found a very pretty replacement – even if she didn't know anything about driving or horses. She soon proved that at least she was happy talking to people.

The trip was a great success.

I met the girl again a few days later when she drove past in her old Morris Minor car. She told me that she had just passed her driving test and was looking for a job. I told her to come and see me. That was the start of Nicky Gaisford. She has helped us for many years; although she has left now and again, she keeps returning.

It was proving to be a very stormy winter. Just before Christmas an Irish rugby player and his German girlfriend asked me to take them out to Postbridge. We were, as usual, very short of cash and I was keen to do the trip if at all possible.

Rose, Nicky's daughter, was quite young and as there was nobody at home to look after her she had to come with us. We knew from the weather forecast that the weather was likely to turn rough. We put waterproof rugs on the cart and took a bottle of farm-made Calvados that we had left from our trip to France earlier in the year. I thought that a few tots might help to keep the customers happy.

All went well until we passed the Cator Strips, a wood high on the moor. The gale hit us with such force I had to ask them to sit on the windward side to stop us being blown over. The reins were being blown out in a semi circle. Lots of Calvados was called for. We arrived at *The East Dart Hotel* at Postbridge and put the horses in the stables. The Irishman filled us up with Guinness and whisky chasers. He was also quite a magician and kept doing conjuring tricks, much to Rose's delight.

The weather outside sounded awful, but in the end we just had to brave it back across the moor. It was a good job that the horses knew the way home. Maggie met us as we came into Holne. She was worried and driving out to look for us as we were so late. We were all tired and wet – but at least we had a bit of cash for Christmas.

We were asked to attend a country sports fair being held at Cherry Brook, the other side of Tavistock. I suppose that it is over twenty miles away on the other side of Dartmoor and we had no lorry or trailer, so if we were going we would have to get there by horse-power. I decided to take the team of Dartmoors. My youngest helper was Nicky Bragg, who was still at school. She drove Woolley to an exercise cart. Although Woolley is only about eleven hands he kept up well. Lynn, who was working for me that winter, drove her cob along behind, but he seemed to be making heavy work of the hills. To add to our difficulties the Dartmoor fog suddenly came down. This made the crossing of the moor a bit hazardous.

After we had made it across the moor we stopped for a well-earned rest beside the road near Moorshop, the site of what used to be a blacksmith's shop. While we were parked there a local farmer came along and in no uncertain terms told us to clear off. He thought that we were a bunch of hippies who were about to invade his fields. He was OK after I explained who we were and what we were doing.

We arrived at Mr and Mrs James' farm close to the showground, where we had arranged to leave the ponies overnight while we went home by car. The James family are famous for their shire horses.

When we finally arrived at the showground next day we were given a great welcome as the commentator told the crowd how we had driven across the moor to support the show.

Nicky Bragg, who was only about fifteen at the time, wanted to drive the team in the ring. I knew that she was quite capable of doing this with a little bit of support, so I sat beside her while she did a driving display doing some figure of eights and a slalom around the cones. I don't think that she hit any of them over. This was a terrific achievement for such a young girl.

As soon as we had done our bit for the show we set off on the long drive home across Dartmoor. There is a very long steep hill out of Tavistock that really tested the ponies, but we had an ice cream stop at the top of the hill while they rested. There is a terrific view right down to the sea at Plymouth and away down into Cornwall.

We passed the famous Dartmoor Prison at Princetown. The road is much easier from there on until Huccaby Hill after crossing the narrow stone bridge over the West Dart.

This is a very steep hill with great big S bends all the way up. It is a terrific test for any horses or ponies to tackle. Jolly Lane Cottage is about half way up the hill. This cottage is reputed to be the last house built on Dartmoor under 'settler's rights' which meant that it had to be built in a day to secure ownership. It had to have a roof on it, and smoke coming out of the chimney, by nightfall for the settler to be successful.

Nicky Gaisford and her husband were the tenants of this cottage until a fire made it uninhabitable.

We still had to battle up the steep hill after crossing the O Brook up to Combestone Tor. From there it is mostly downhill to home. It felt a long, long trip.

Margaret Gardiner bought a Welsh cob called Bimbo that had previously been in an FEI team owned by David Brand and competed at top national level. She was keen to find out how he went in harness and asked me to take a look at him. I decided to put him in as a pair with our old cob, Munnings. So many of these ex-competition horses can be a real handful, as they tend to get very hotted up. I thought Munnings would steady him.

I was right, Bimbo shot out of the yard in a series of frightening leaps, dragging Munnings with him. Having got him a bit settled, we decided to drive them to Postbridge. Bimbo pulled like a train all the way there.

We were just sitting down for lunch in the pub when Nicky realised that she hadn't arranged for anyone to collect Rose from school in Widecombe. She couldn't get hold of anyone by phone to do it, so the only solution was for us to drive the pair to Widecombe. Once again Bimbo pulled his heart out, but Munnings was playing the "I am an old horse" game and not doing so very much. We collected Rose on time.

As soon as he realised we were heading for home, Munnings woke up and set off with a will, dragging the exhausted Bimbo beside him. Bimbo was never so wild again.

We decided to go to a cross-country driving event that was being held near South Molton. Brian Townsend, who was a chef from Birmingham and a long-standing customer, came with me.

We drove right across Dartmoor, going up Dr Blackall's carriage drive. This is a rough old track high above the Dart Valley that was built many years ago for the good doctor's wife. It has been allowed to get very rough. In fact, it is a real cross-country test in itself.

We went past Cator and on up the magnificent Challacombe valley, past my birthplace at Stiniel and down Meldon to Chagford, where we had a drink at *The Three Crowns* before continuing on our way. We went through the Gidleigh Park Hotel grounds and past the old Gidleigh Castle to Moortown Gate. We put the ponies up overnight at Taw Green. Maggie collected us with a car and took us back next day to continue our journey.

We went through North Tawton to Bondleigh and on to Eggesford Station where we joined the A377 and followed it to the junction with the B3226 and then on to South Molton where we stayed on a farm owned by Jackie Shapland's partner. Jackie had been on the last course that I had run at Stinhall when I had met Maggie. She also came to Michelcombe several times. Sadly, I haven't seen her for many years.

Oddly enough, I am afraid that I am unable to remember much about the competition except the terrific reception we got as we arrived. The crowd had been told about our long drive to get there. This had to be one of the longest drives I ever attempted, over forty miles in each direction. Of course, we still had to drive home which we did by the same route. Nowadays we just couldn't find the time for such an adventure.

I had broken in a grey horse for a Mr Tucker, a well-known coaching farmer and dealer. He had bought a farm by the seaside during the war, but had turned it into caravan sites when the war was over. He was reputed to be very wealthy, but he certainly didn't like parting with any cash. In fact, I refused to do any more work for him. He had an old genuine road coach on the road and did some very long trips right across the country. One day he rang me up to offer us a ride on his coach. I was rather pleased as I thought it was something of an honour.

Maggie and I arranged to meet the coach at Red Cross on the A3072 between Bude and Holsworthy. What a magnificent sight the coach and horses made as they swung down the hill towards us. I could see the horse that I had broken was being used as a leader. I was expecting to ride as a passenger, but Bill insisted that I took on the driving. At first I felt honoured by this, but I gradually realised that Bill had got me up to drive the coach as he had injured an arm and couldn't drive himself. By inviting me as a guest I became one of his unpaid staff for the day. He later sold the horse that I had broken for a small fortune, but I think he managed to forget the promise of extra money to me if he made a good sale.

I drove them all day. We went through Holsworthy and onto the A388. We pulled up at a farm that was owned by a dealer friend of the Tuckers. There was quite a party that night, but we had to leave early as I had customers the next day.

Speaking of driving spectacular coaches reminds me that for my 70th birthday, Carolyn Owen, who has been a regular customer and friend for many years, treated me to a morning's driving with John Parker in Norfolk.

John, who is President of the British Driving Society and one of the top coachmen in the world, showed us around his collection of coaches and carriages, and asked me about my experience of team driving. Although I have been driving teams of ponies and horses for many years now, I use the Hungarian method of rein handling, and all of our carriages have brakes fitted which is very different from the coaching style of driving which is used on many of John's carriages and coaches. So when it came to going out for a drive I was thrilled to see that it was to be his Norwich Union Coach; and even more so when he allowed me to drive it, with him sitting next to me offering advice.

The drive took us through the open countryside of Norfolk, giving us great views from up on the coach. Not that I had time to admire them – I was totally concentrating on my horses as this coach requires a very different driving technique. Even the slightest slope had to be so accurately driven, but with John's help I gained confidence as we went on.

All too soon we were back in his yard. I felt very honoured when he told me that I was only the fifth man to have driven the coach since the 1920s. What a day to remember – thank you Carolyn.

Jonathan Mathys asked us to do a long trip around the South Hams. We took the pony team to the coach and Munnings to an exercise cart. The first leg was to Marion Ash's at Beenleigh Manor, Diptford, where we left the ponies overnight. We stayed with Jonathan in Totnes. We then made our way along a number of green lanes to Aveton Gifford where we went along the tidal road that runs alongside the River Avon. The tide was going out, but the water still covered the road. The road was indicated by poles sticking out of the water. Our guide assured us that it wouldn't be too deep – but my little leader, Woolley, was swimming at one spot! We reached Bigbury-on-Sea and went out across the beach to *The Pilchard,* the pub on Burgh Island. We nearly got stuck coming back as the narrow traditional wheels on the coach cut deep into the sand, although Munnings and his exercise cart with car wheels was all right. We stayed that night at a farm near Kingston. We made it back home the next day, but it was a very long drive and it had been a hard trip.

For many years now we have provided carriage rides at Scorriton Flower Show. We used to take the pony team, but since the arrival of Mr Allen and Badger they have done this show. We do as many trips as possible up and down the showground. I find it a bit boring, but we manage to earn quite a lot of money for the show and charity. The show committee presents us with a huge bowl of mixed fruit around Christmas time. Once we have done Scorriton, which takes place on the August Bank Holiday weekend, we know that we are getting close to the end of our summer season.

We always do a number of picnic trips for clients during the summer months. Usually we provide the eats, but some customers like to bring their own. A couple who were staying at an upmarket hotel recently turned up with a picnic provided by the hotel. It had cost them £36 and consisted of a piece of cake, a couple of very ordinary sandwiches and some fruit. I would have described it as a poor working man's lunch.

The other side of the coin was a picnic provided by a party of ladies that I took on the last trip before I had a serious accident. The weather was superb. We did a full Postbridge trip of over thirty miles and stopped at the Walla Brook where there is a lovely picnic spot. The ladies provided a really luxurious beanfeast.

We are doing more picnic trips nowadays as the pubs can be so slow in serving food that it makes the lunch break too long and means that we are late back for our staff. Some pubs are not always as helpful as they might be, I'm sorry to say.

I sometimes act as a guide for people who bring their own horses to ride on the moor. I showed Sophie White and a friend of hers the safe path through the bogs called Sandy Way. The route follows that of an old packhorse route to Princetown. We came home following the Ashburton pack road, which is sometimes called by locals 'The Conchie Road', as it was worked on by Conscientious Objectors during the war. I found that the track had been improved by the farmer.

When I saw this I decided to try and drive a team over to Princetown using this bridle path. I took with me Barbara Norman and Carolyn Owen. I was barely able to walk after snapping an Achilles tendon in a fall.

All went well until we crossed the Swincombe River, but going up through the abandoned farm the track became very rough and the pole broke. So there I was, stuck, with me crippled and two ladies. Carolyn had a mobile phone and tried to ring home, but only got the answering machine. I always carry rope and some spare harness, but not a spare pole. Luckily Mike, who was working for us then and had stayed at home that day to do other work, had picked up a rather garbled message (mobile reception isn't good on Dartmoor), and guessed what had happened. He loaded up a spare pole and the necessary tools and drove out to meet us as near as he could on the road.

But Lady Luck came to our rescue in the form of a group of strong young men who appeared walking towards us along the track. They readily agreed to help and used the rope to tow and steer the wagon back to a concrete road used by the water board, and from there on to the public road at Sherburton. I had to ride on the wagon to work the brakes. We met Mike and quickly changed poles and drove to *The Forest Inn* where I bought everyone a drink.

*

I liked the idea of arranging a drive to resemble a coach journey, such as the Mail Coaches used to do. I worked out a route that took us to a number of pubs where we could change passengers and some of the team.

We tried it for the first time in 1995 and used a waggonette that I had designed and had made in Buckfast by Rod Mortimore. I still have it to this day. It performs beautifully and I've just fitted a new set of spoked steel wheels from Poland.

I didn't have enough ponies or helpers to make a complete change at each stop, but the stops were only a few miles apart. I thought that changing some of the team at a couple of stops would add to the atmosphere. I arranged for the passenger changes and for the delivery and collection of the ponies.

We started from a local pub, *The Tradesman's Arms* in Scorriton, where the landlord and his wife gave us a good send off. Our first stop was at *The Church House Inn* at Holne where we picked up some more passengers.

We set off across Holne Moor. There are some lovely views on this route as we cross Venford Reservoir, with a steep pull afterwards. We passed Deadman's Pit and Combestone Tor. We were very glad that we had hydraulic brakes on all four wheels as we went down the steep hill to Saddle Bridge. The ponies pulled well up the hill on the other side.

Our next stop was at *The Forest Inn*, Hexworthy, where we changed passengers before setting off for Two Bridges. We had to go down the steep Huccaby Hill with its great sweeping turns, past the famous Jolly Lane Cottage and on over the high granite arched bridge that spans the West Dart.

On reaching the main road we turned left. From there the road is much better for the ponies. The newtake on the right was where the famous Huccaby Races were held before the war. This was a flat race meeting held under the now defunct Pony Turf Club rules. I have an advertising poster dated 1927. I have never seen much written about these races and all the old people who were involved have now passed on.

We crossed the little bridge at Dunnabridge and swept up around the bends passing the old point-to-point course on our right. I can honestly claim to have ridden a winner here before I was born – I even have a picture of Mother to prove it. I also rode a horse called Timosity to a brilliant win, beating Prince Blackthorn who had won the Cheltenham Gold Cup some years before. I also fell off Dundee here when he was a hot favourite – not so clever!

We crossed the Cherry Brook and sprung the hill after it. It is then a level run onto Two Bridges where we changed both the passengers and our leader ponies. The new ponies were a bit green, so this next stage was ideal for them as it's pretty straightforward. We passed Parson's Cottage. It used to be called Billy Clack's house. He was the parson at Moretonhampstead and an early Master of the Mid Devon Hunt.

We passed the long-disused gunpowder factory and went down across The Hairy Hands Bridge, where hairy hands are supposed to grab the reins (or your steering wheel) and turn you over! Whoever owns them must have been asleep as we got across quite safely.

We soon dropped down into Postbridge where a big crowd was awaiting us. We had a proper stop at *The East Dart Hotel* for lunch and then we put two leader ponies on to make a six-in-hand. We had to fit an extra pole for the swing ponies, just as they do in the John Wayne stagecoach movies.

Previously I just used to hook the traces from horse to horse as the King's Troop RHA do. We then had to tackle Merripit Hill. I hadn't ever taken a team up there before. It looks a very long drag from the bottom, but I needn't have worried as the ponies seemed to be able to manage a lot more power using the extra pole. We made it to the top without having either to stop or unload passengers. What a terrific view lay all around us from the top of this hill. I pulled over to the side of the road in order to give the ponies a blow, but they soon wanted to be gone again.

So on we went, down the other side of the hill to cross Stats Bridge. Stats House is an old ruin of a house close by.

We pulled up the hill to *The Warren House Inn*. This is the third highest pub in the U.K. and has a fire that is reputed not to have gone out for some one hundred and fifty years. Of course, it used to be a peat fire. About one hundred years ago the pub was moved from one side of the road to the other and the fire was carried across the road on a shovel. This was a miners' pub that served the Vitifer Mines. At their peak close to two hundred people worked in this area.

After another change of passengers, and more changing of ponies, we set off for Beetor Cross that was to be our last stop before Chagford. We passed the lonely Bennett's Cross that used to mark the way across the moor and pulled up Birch Tor hill. From here we could see all the way to Exmoor and both Meldon and Nattadon hills just outside Chagford. Just before Beetor Cross there is a stone cross on the wall that is called Watching Place. This is where people waited for the Mail coach that used to run right across the moor on the route that we had been following from Two Bridges. Once again there was a good crowd of supporters waiting for us.

We did some more changes before we left. Rose Gaisford, who was only about fifteen, took on the driving to the outskirts of Chagford. We had to pass my old birthplace and childhood home of Stiniel. I couldn't help wondering if Mother and Father were watching from somewhere.

I had arranged with Anne Williams, famous for her work with shire horses, that she would collect the ponies with her horsebox. She was waiting for us in the car park at the back of the Jubilee Hall. We made sure that the ponies were comfortable after their journey and then we all headed for *The Three Crowns Hotel* where Mr and Mrs Giles, the long-serving landlord and landlady, awaited us. We had quite a celebration – especially as I wasn't driving home.

The following year we decided to do another journey via Chagford. I found that Anne Williams would be away at a ploughing match with her magnificent pair of shires. This meant that we didn't have the use of her lorry, so I decided to drive the team to Chagford and leave them overnight with my long time friend, Mick McGlyn, at Easton Cross.

We decided to use the six-in-hand all the way, which meant that we didn't have to bother with changes. As there would be no passengers to pick up on the way to Chagford, we didn't have to be anywhere by set times, so we could go at whatever pace we liked. That meant that I could give some of our helpers the chance to drive the team on quiet roads.

We had a nice leisurely drive going by way of Holne and crossing the Dart at New Bridge. Here I unloaded my helpers, who were taken up the long steep hill by car. Then with one helper as groom we turned left and stormed up the hill through Hannaford. This is an extremely steep hill, but there are several places where it is possible to stop and give the ponies a breather. I galloped them up the steepest bits.

My God, what a buzz a team of six galloping ponies gives me!

We kept stopping on the level bits. Our last stop was outside the Methodist Chapel after Poundsgate. Then there is a last pull up to the top of the hill to Butts Cross. We turned off onto the Bellever road. Once we had got up there the going is much better with only gentle hills to cope with. We trotted on past Anne William's farm at Corndonford, where her dogs gave us a great welcome.

We then made our way through Cator and drove up to Mr Irish's farm along his farm drive. This brought us out onto the Straight Mile at the bottom of the Challacombe Valley. This is a spectacular valley that has a lot of history attached to it. There used to be a medieval village there that was wiped out by the Black Death.

Big terraces run along both sides of the valley. I like to think that they were used to grow grapes to make wine for the miners – but that is probably just my wishful thinking.

Next we passed the entrance to Headland Warren. I am told that this lonely farm used to be a pub for the miners. We then passed the site of Grimspound, a Bronze Age walled village. As we crested the head of the valley we could see all the way to Exmoor in front of us and behind us stretched the long valley looking out over the South Hams towards the sea. It is then downhill to Beetor, up the hill beside Stiniel, down Meldon Hill, through the centre of Chagford and down to Easton Cross, where we left the ponies with Mick McGlyn.

We returned next morning to make an early start. We caught up, brushed and harnessed the ponies in readiness for the long drive home. As we were putting to, Brian Townsend's little dog jumped up onto the seat next to me and started to bark. For some reason all the ponies got very upset and all hell broke loose. Ponies were plunging about more like unbroken ponies than a well-made team. They managed to break several pieces of harness. I always carry some spare bits of harness and lots of plastic baler cord. I used up all of these spares trying to get the whole outfit back on the road.

I had just got the team settled and trotting down the road when we met the Mid Devon Hunt galloping by in full cry. What with the horn blowing and the pack of hounds in good voice, this was all I needed! However, the members of the hunt had much more trouble with their horses than I did with the team. Mind you, two of my ponies, Pip and Dodger, had both been hunting with Rose with the Dartmoor Hounds and they got quite excited.

We drove up through Chagford and went into the yard of *The Three Crowns* where we had arranged to pick up our first lot of passengers. When we had loaded up we came out under the arch only to find that some cars were parked just where we wanted to turn right, so I had to have a quick change of plan and do a left turn and then go right around the pepper pot building in the middle of the Square. This makes for a very sharp turn and a totally unhelpful milkman did not help things. These difficulties having been overcome, we clattered off down New Street. The ponies had settled down well, but when they saw Meldon Hill with its steep winding turns they really started to pull my arms out of their sockets. These guys just love storming up these steep hills. We made it to the top of Meldon without having to stop and unload passengers.

We trotted on back past Stiniel and down to Beetor Bridge where it crosses the River Bovey. There is an old mill dam across the river here where we used to swim as boys.

Then we tackled the steep, twisty, narrow road up to Beetor Cross where our next lot of passengers was awaiting us. We had a short break before we attempted the terrific hills up to Bush Down, right on top of the moor.

I wasn't at all sure that the ponies would be able to cope with the hill out of Green Coombe. There was only one way to find out – by having a go. I warned my passengers that they might have to get out and walk. As we tackled this hill, a bus came up behind us. I asked the ponies for a final burst up the hill. They gave me a terrific response and galloped clean away from the bus.

We stopped on the top of Bush Down to give the ponies a well-earned breather. We had lots of cheers and hand-waving from the bus passengers when they caught up with us.

Then it was on past Bennett's Cross to our next stop at the *Warren House Inn* where we changed passengers again. We had got there a bit early and had to wait for some passengers – I always thought that it was the passengers that did the waiting!

We were soon on our way again to our next stop at *The East Dart Hotel* at Postbridge. Here we took the ponies out and gave them a feed in the stables while we all had lunch there. I was strictly on the Diet Coke, as these journeys are such a responsibility.

We put to and set off again over the East Dart River with the ancient clapper bridge. There is a little petrol station that sells the best pasties on Dartmoor on the right. Just past this shop is the farm where the old Mail coaches used to change horses. On we went, leaving Bellever Woods to our left and down to the Hairy Hands Bridge. Having crossed this bridge (without any mishap!) we headed off for our next stop at *The Two Bridges Hotel* where we changed passengers yet again. As we breasted the hill after the Hotel we were then heading straight for home and the ponies certainly knew it. We really barrelled along over the Cherry Brook Bridge and the old Dunnabridge racecourse. After leaving the main road we crossed the very narrow Huccaby Bridge which feels a mile high from the box seat. We then came to Huccaby Hill, which is by far the most challenging hill on the whole route with its great sweeping steep bends. It is a really formidable challenge. Well, of course, the ponies wouldn't think of letting me down, but as we stormed up the hill we met a motorist coming towards us. He stopped in the middle of the road and just froze. I was able to squeeze by him, just avoiding the ditch at the side of the road. It made me a bit nervous – what it did to the motorist I can't imagine. So it was into *The Forest Inn* for another stop.

As we had the long steep hill to get up from Saddle Bridge to Combestone Tor we didn't carry any passengers for this stage, but picked them up at the Tor for our last, mostly downhill, stage.

Even after such a long journey the ponies didn't seem tired.

So it was back to home successfully to where all of our passengers and supporters had gathered to await our arrival.

We had a terrific party that we held in the alleyway of the stables. Maggie cooked supper for about fifty of us; John French brought in a barrel of his home-made cider and also provided music with his guitar.

We repeated the whole exercise the following year. As it had all worked well, we followed the same pattern. This was a shirtsleeve-order journey all the way. As it was so hot I set a very gentle pace to help the ponies and did, indeed, walk a lot of the way. This gave us plenty of time to talk about the moor and see the wonderful views. We certainly didn't break any speed records.

In 1999 we did the last of these journeys. We had good weather going up to Chagford, but it was a different story the next day. We put to in pouring rain. In fact, it rained hard the whole way. Amazingly, we had a full complement of passengers who, without exception, took it all in good part. As we crested Bush Down on the way to *The Warren House Inn* we were hit by a terrible hailstorm. It blew into our faces with full fury. I was worried that my leaders might try to turn around, but they didn't let me down and faced up to the fury of the storm. Conditions got better after we left Two Bridges as the wind was then behind us and the worst of the rain and hail had eased off. These were some of the worst weather conditions that I had ever met on Dartmoor. Vida Alexander was my groom on that day and was her usual efficient self.

We were really ready for the party that night.

We haven't attempted this journey again. I have never

heard of anybody, either before or since, who has done anything like this with a team of six Dartmoor ponies on a commercial basis.

*

As soon as we had the new coach built I was really keen to trial it on some trips.

We took it to Princetown for the Dartmoor Jailbreak Charity event for Vida Alexander and her family. While turning in the prison yard I nearly turned it over by turning too short and locking the front wheels on the perch. Only by chance Maggie was standing in the right place and managed to hold it upright. How she ever found the strength to do it I shall never know!

For its first serious run we asked Anne Williams to transport us up to Wheddon Cross on Exmoor. As was often the case, it poured with rain, and being in April it was rather chilly, but we carried on. The route we followed was largely downhill following the River Exe through this beautiful valley. The ponies made light work of the trip and we trotted nearly all the way. There was little motor traffic on the road, but there was lots of wildlife to be seen as we trotted by. The weather cleared up a bit for us. As arranged we stopped at a lay-by close to Tiverton where Annie and her lorry were waiting for us. The lorry has living accommodation so we could have a very welcome cup of tea and some soup.

For the next trip we headed for *The East Dart* at Postbridge. As the hills are so steep we put Mr Allen and Badger in the wheel and four ponies in front of them. It made a long team to get through the top gate at Spitchwick Park and I was a bit lucky to get through without mishap. The weather was wet again, but it cleared up as the day went on. We all had a good lunch at the pub and came home in a happy state. This trip was a good test of the coach and my ability to drive it.

The next year Vida Alexander got us a job with the coach in Kingsbridge. We had to take some schoolchildren from the old railway yard up the steep main street to the Cookworthy Museum. We put Mr Allen and Badger in the wheel and Pip and

Vodka as leaders. I was worried that we might be a bit overloaded, but we had no problems – the team just flew up the steep hill. We were supposed to have a motorcycle police escort, but one never appeared. Neil Watts and Vida were the grooms, with Maggie doing her usual back-up with the car.

A few weeks later Maggie and I went in the car to Clovelly in North Devon. We decided to drive there using minor roads and by doing so we found a possible coach route in the Lydford and Bridestowe area. We went back there another day and mapped a route from *The Fox and Hounds* on the main Okehampton road, past Coryton, on to Portgate, onto the old A30 right-handed through Lewdown to Bridestowe. Once again Annie kindly volunteered the use of her lorry to move the team while we took the coach on our new trailer. We all arrived at *The Fox and Hounds* and were soon on the road, following the planned route. For a change we had good weather. There was almost no traffic, bluebells in the woods and buzzards overhead. I remember that we passed two smart grey cobs playing in a field and they seemed quite keen to join us.

We had a video cameraman taking shots of us for The Friends of the Dartmoor Hill Pony group. There was a stiff climb up onto the old A30, on through Lewdown to Bridestowe, where we gave the ponies a break before tackling the return trip to *The Fox and Hounds* where the landlord had lunch waiting. We had a large crowd of supporters who joined us for what proved to be a lovely, memorable day.

*

I've mentioned Shirley and Bob McKennee before, but not yet described my trip to them in America.

During their visits to us Shirley became very fond of our Dartmoors and she decided that she would like to buy a pair to take home. However, she wanted pure-bred Dartmoors whereas all our ponies are Moorland stock so we had to look elsewhere.

I would never have believed that this would prove to be such a difficult task. Shirley wanted plain bay geldings of about five years of age. We found a suitable pony nearby at Dunsford, but then we had to scour the length and breadth of the country looking for another.

We tried through the Dartmoor Pony Society, but nobody had such a pony for sale. I remember that a dealer way down in Cornwall had one advertised for sale. I phoned, told him exactly what we were looking for and he claimed that he had just what we wanted. We travelled to see it and I was very angry when he produced a black pony.

Eventually we found a pony at Exeter belonging to a well-known dealer and riding stable owner. We went to see him. I was not happy with his front feet, but as he had to be vetted I asked the vet to pay particular attention to his feet. The vet passed him as sound. Soon after we got him home we had to have him shod by our farrier. He told us that the pony had had laminitis. All the tell tale rings around his hooves had been rasped off to remove obvious signs. My God, what a mess! If only I had gone by my own gut feeling.

Robbie Richardson, who lives in our hamlet, was working as a referral farrier. He put in a lot of work and succeeded in getting this pony sound.

We trained the two ponies to go single and as a pair; then they were flown to America from Stansted.

A year later, Shirley was having troubles with them and asked me to go out there to sort the problem. I had never been to America, in fact I'd never even been to Heathrow before – what a terrifying place that is!

When I arrived at Kennedy Airport I had to fill in a yellow form. I had been told that if I didn't get it right I wouldn't be allowed in. I queued up at a desk with a lot of black people in front of me who seemed to be on the receiving end of some rough treatment from the immigration officers. By the time I got to the desk I was really nervous, but they just glanced at the form and waved me by.

I was pleased to see Bob waiting to meet me. We went along a huge toll-paying motorway through Connecticut at a steady fifty miles an hour and arrived at their house near Washington Depot. This is lovely wooded country with very little traffic compared to our roads back home.

Shirley had just taken delivery of a brand new Bennington

waggonette from England. She had a brand new set of pairs harness from Smuckers, an American firm that I believe are of the Amish religion. Shirley seemed to have several American ladies who were giving her different advice and so nothing was going right. Although she had asked me to sort it out, she didn't seem to want to listen to me. In the end, I rather blew my top and told her to either let me do my job or send me back home. She'd been trying to work the pair without any help except for Bob. As the ponies were still a bit green, she had an artificial leg and Bob was an elderly man, this was asking too much.

We drove the ponies into Washington Depot. It was fairly flat going, but as we drove into the top end of town we started to go downhill and the brakes completely failed to work. The breeching didn't work because it didn't fit. I had told Shirley about this and asked her to get some more holes put in it, but she'd said that as it was made especially for her ponies I must be wrong. As we started down the hill the carriage ran into the back legs of the ponies that promptly ran away with the carriage running into them. I managed to weave my way through the town traffic and found a bit of uphill road to stop them on.

One of the ponies had kicked his leg over the traces. I was trying to get it back over when he kicked me hard on the knee. I thought that he had broken it. Somehow I managed to drive them back home.

Shirley gave me some of the hottest liniment I have ever used to put on the knee. I awoke in the night thinking that my whole leg was on fire. Amazingly it made my leg much better by next day.

I had to find out why the brakes had completely failed, find and train a girl groom and have the harness sorted out. We got some friends of Shirley to pull the waggonette by hand. I kept trying the brakes with the hand lever in different positions. There was no 'on' or 'off' marked, but I found out that there was a third position which shut off the brakes, but let the wheels go round. I had only ever come across brakes that were either on or off, so this was a surprise.

There are miles of gravel roads in the area, such as there were in Britain between the wars. We only had brakes on the back wheels. With only Bob on the back the wheels just slid along if we tried to go down some of the steep hills. After taking the ponies out for some more trips I was worried by the awful noises coming from the fifth wheel. I contacted the American rep for Bennington about these problems. He told me that it was impossible to fit brakes on the front. I knew that this was nonsense as I had a cart made by a local garage that had such brakes and that they worked very well on similar road surfaces. As for the noises, he said that the box seat was acting like a violin and if we filled it up with blankets the noise would stop. This certainly reduced the noise, but I was still concerned that the fifth wheel was failing.

Shirley took me out in the evening to meet her friends, who were all very upmarket. We went for dinner with the President of the American Driving Society. He buttonholed me as soon as we arrived and wheeled me into his coach house. He gave me the third degree and asked me every question he could think of. I must have coped all right because he was impressed enough to offer me a drive the next morning of his four-in-hand of Lipizzaners.

I had a lovely drive with these magnificent horses. We were going along a beautiful valley on a dirt road that I thought was on his estate, when a huge timber lorry roared past us. There was a high drop down right beside us. I was frightened that the horses would jump down it, but they were as steady as a rock. He explained that many of the public roads in New England were dirt roads. It was a truly memorable drive in this lovely countryside.

On another evening I was taken to a stud farm. The owner played a little game on me. She took me down to her barn (that we would call stables) and led a big pony out of a box. She asked me what breed I thought it was. To me it was a big Dartmoor pony such as we used to see years ago being ridden by Dartmoor farmers about their stock.

To my surprise she told me that it was a Morgan of the old type. Up until then the only Morgans that I had seen were of the park type, just small, lightweight thoroughbreds. I had often wondered how these little horses had been cavalry horses or farm horses.

On another evening I was invited to a very grand estate in

the Berkshire Mountains. There was a long drive up to the house. As we arrived a beautiful lady walked down the flight of steps to great us. The setting sun was behind her. The dress she had on was rather filmy; the view was interesting. During the course of the meal she asked me if I knew Bertie Hill. I knew Bertie well, of course. We were amateur jockeys at the same time and he went on to win an equestrian Olympic gold medal. Once that had been established, she was more than impressed.

I also met an Englishman who was trying to make it in the American horse world. I'm afraid I can't remember his name. I believe he had worked in The Royal Mews before going to America. On the way back from his stables Shirley said that we could call in at a basement that sold harness, saddlery and carriages. She also mentioned that the girl who ran it wasn't very helpful.

My idea of a basement was an underground room beneath a house. How wrong I was; it was a huge store with a wonderful selection of everything. The girl turned out to be a charming, attractive, blonde young lady who couldn't have been more helpful. She had a super-looking cross-country cart for sale, which could be supplied in any size or colour with brakes on all four wheels and this was just a few miles down the road! I couldn't understand why Shirley hadn't bought one of those. I would have loved to bring home one of those carts with a set of their harness. I might have taken the young lady as well, but that would have got me into trouble.

I had done my best to sort out the problems and it was time for the long flight home. During the flight I was thinking about the Morgans that I had seen, when I made the connection between the Morgan and the, now probably extinct, Devon Pack Horse. They were the same height, colour and type and had the same performance.

It had been a great experience, but I was glad to be back on Dartmoor.

*

Colin Henderson was involved in organising a driving trial at Cirencester and asked me to go up there. I had spent years living in the Cirencester area so it was a bit like going home.

We took Pip and Dodger as a pair and Maggie took her mare Solo. It was a long time since I had done any competition driving.

When we were getting ready a man came up to me and assured me that, "Your ponies won't be fast enough nowadays."

I didn't rise to the bait. I knew that they would go a good trot. It was one of those events where everything went well and I won the pairs class.

Willie Carson, the famous jockey, presented the prizes.

It was the last competition I entered. May as well end on a winning note.

CHAPTER 12

Foot-and-mouth; accidents; very useful help

The outbreak of foot-and-mouth disease in 2001 was dreadful. All the cattle and sheep that ran on the moor and the farms around Hexworthy were shot and burned in huge bonfires that were shown on national television.

Although we don't have any livestock that can catch the dreaded disease, we weren't allowed to ride a horse across the moor to feed the ponies that we had in the Knapp (fields that we rent in a valley within the moor). We were, however, allowed to take our ancient Ferguson tractor. As there was no proper track the tractor was creating ruts and causing damage. The National Park Authority started to object and I rather jokingly told them to build me a road.

To my complete surprise they agreed to do it. They turned up with great big diggers, dumper trucks and lorry loads of stone. They really cut up the moor far worse than my old tractor would have done, but in the end we were left with a useful track.

The fencing around the Knapp was in a very poor state. The moorland sheep were always breaking in. Our landlord was very reluctant to make good this fence which hadn't had any serious repairs for some forty years. We were very worried as the authorities were threatening to have all the wild moorland ponies shot as they might be carriers of the disease. We had a lot of trained young *Dartmoor Driving* ponies running up there. The only hope was to make good the fence ourselves.

I went to Tuckers and bought loads of stakes and wire. Peter Dodd, who has helped us at weekends for some twenty years and is a fencing expert, came and gave me a hand. I still had to spend many days in cold, wet weather working on the fence.

One particularly cold, wet day I was waiting for Peter to carry some stakes up to me and I was looking at the ancient deer bank and ditch. These banks have a deep ditch on the moorland side, but were sloped on the field side in order that any deer could be chased out. They date back to the days when there were herds of wild deer running on the moor (there still are a few in the wooded valleys). I was idly wondering about the men who originally built these great earthworks. I let my mind drift back to those times, so many years ago, and I made up a story about the construction of the bank.

When I got home I wrote it down, Maggie typed it out and printed it, and we sent it off to *Carriage Driving Monthly* magazine. I had never written anything before, but to my delight and amazement they actually published it. This was to start a whole new line of work for me as they have published many other articles of mine since.

It was some time before we were allowed to take horses and carriages onto the moorland roads, but eventually this awful nightmare came to an end and we were able to resume normal work – which meant doing a mixture of serious carriage driving training and holiday trips, where I drive a group of visitors, tell them all about Dartmoor and try to encourage them to take an interest in driving with an eye to future trade.

We still do the occasional wedding. I also used to take horses to train for driving, but I'm getting a bit long in the tooth for this job and certainly don't have the time in the summer.

*

Over the years I feel I have had more than my fair share of accidents. In fact, I've had so many that I struggle to remember them all.

I've already described the serious one when I broke both jaws as a teenage jockey. There followed several broken legs and arms, mostly as a result of horse related accidents, but also when no horses were involved. Sometimes there was no one involved but me.

For example, one day I was looking at an exhibition of photographs in St Anne's Chapel in Ashburton when I fell down a step I just didn't see. At first I thought I'd broken my leg, but gradually the pain subsided. I had left the dogs in the back of my pick-up and was worried that they might jump out if I left them for too long, so I struggled outside and somehow managed to get home. I got Mike Oborn, who was working here at the time, to run me to Torbay Hospital. They told me that I had snapped an Achilles tendon and plastered me up. It was eventually cured by a very good lady osteopath.

Once when I was driving a straw lorry, I had to pull up in a lay-by to adjust a sheet that was flapping in the wind. One of the sheet ropes had a metal end that hit me in the eye. The pain was unbelievable and for some reason it affected the other eye, too. So there I was, stuck in a lay-by, unable to see at all. Luckily I was able to wave down another lorry and explained what had happened. The driver took me to the local hospital and helped me inside. I was off work for several weeks before the eye healed up.

By far the worst of my accidents was when a customer that I was teaching to drive a pair drove into the hedge. I yelled to her that she was too close, but either I was a bit late or she didn't react quickly enough. The carriage rolled over and a wheel nearly severed my right leg, just below the knee. At first I had no idea how serious the injury was and I tried to get up to look after the ponies. To my horror I could see that my foot was hanging the wrong way. I collapsed back onto the road. A very kindly young lady, who I didn't know, put my head on her lap while the mess was sorted out.

It wasn't too long before the ambulance and police arrived, along with help from Jimmy Frost's racing stable. The ambulance men decided that they needed a helicopter to move me. This seemed to take forever to come to my rescue, as it had been busy elsewhere. I had been conscious all the time and the pain was becoming unbearable.

While I was lying in the road I heard one of Jimmy's lads say, "My uncle broke his leg just like that – and he died."

The helicopter landed in the nearest field, but when they tried to stretcher me over to it they found that the gate was locked. The ambulance men were having a job lifting me over it and I had to point out that the gate would lift off its hinges, even though the catch was locked.

I was so relieved to arrive at Derriford Hospital and get the leg sorted. The doctors had to do a lot of skin grafting and luckily that all worked, but the leg didn't set properly and I had to go back into hospital to have it reset. I was very depressed about this as I just hate hospitals. This time they called in an army surgeon, Colonel Rossiter. He was most helpful and explained that he was going to use the elisaroth method to mend my leg. He showed me photographs of other people whose shattered limbs he had repaired. The technique involved having another operation and fixing the bones in place with pins that went right through the leg. The pins were joined together by a frame like a bicycle wheel that went all around my leg.

It worked and I was able to come home soon afterwards. Maggie had arranged for me to have a bed downstairs and set up the microwave on a table within reach so that I could warm food during the day as she was still working full-time at BT in Exeter.

We had a ride-on lawnmower and I had the cutting deck taken off it. This was a great help getting about as it was much more powerful than the electric wheelchair I borrowed that wouldn't go beyond the stables.

I was soon able to get myself up to the village to collect my pension from the Post Office and have a drink in the pub. This made life much better. After one of these expeditions as I limped to the back door I suddenly had an unbelievable pain in my leg. It was agony. I felt as though the metal pins had pulled the bone apart. I somehow managed to crawl back indoors and collapsed on a chair in front of the fire. There was no one about, I couldn't reach the phone and I couldn't bear to move. I just had to wait for Maggie to return from work. When she arrived she called an ambulance. Even with their professional help it was a very painful job to get into the ambulance.

The ambulance nearly got stuck on the humpback bridge at Scorriton. The driver really scraped it getting us over.

I had a very long wait in A & E before anybody could see me. I was waiting in absolute agony while the hospital staff coped with drunks, drug users and people who had been in fights. I had a very bad night, what with the severe pain and worrying as to whether I was going to lose my leg.

In the morning Colonel Rossiter turned up with another naval surgeon. He told the new surgeon to stick a scalpel into my leg. After I had finished yelling, all the pain just went away as the infection poured out. Why the hell couldn't anybody have done that the night before?

There was a very attractive lady Lieutenant-Commander surgeon who had helped with my first operation and who turned up each time that I was in trouble with the leg. The look of her in her uniform made me feel better straight away!

Eventually the great day arrived when they could take the frame off. A junior doctor did it. He wanted me to have yet more anaesthetic, which would have meant yet more time in hospital, but I told him just to get on with it. It was indeed very painful while he unscrewed the pins from my leg. I was determined not to give in as my lady surgeon was looking on.

After this accident I found to my horror that I had lost my nerve when teaching. I was all right when I was driving myself, but that didn't earn any money.

I managed to solve the problem by using two pairs of reins so that the pupil had one set and I still had control when I felt it was needed – just like dual controls in a driving school car.

There was one very strange event in the saga of this injury. One night, as I lay in my hospital bed, I found myself being lifted by four little green men. They took me up to a stone circle on Dartmoor where a tall old man walked around me talking in a language that I didn't understand. When I woke up I was, of course, back in my hospital bed. The odd thing was that I just knew that the skin grafts had finally taken, even though I couldn't see my leg for bandages. When the doctors came round on their morning inspection they were amazed at the improvement.

There was at that time a stone circle painted on the ceiling at the entrance to Derriford Hospital, although I had never noticed it.

Sometime later when I had finally got home, I told my GP, Dr Edwards, the story. To my amazement he didn't laugh it off, but told me that during his long years in practice on the moor he had heard similar tales from other Dartmoor patients.

While I was at home, slowly recovering, I received a phone

call from a warder at Dartmoor Prison. I had previously broken in a driving pony for him. He had heard of my troubles on the grapevine. He told me that there was a prisoner who had previously worked with harness horses. The warder spoke very highly of this man and said that it could be arranged for him to be allowed out during the day to work for us.

Maggie and I went to meet him. We had seen the outside often enough, but we had never been inside Dartmoor Prison. When we arrived it was getting dark and the fog was swirling around the huge gates. We were escorted through the prison by a very big warder and shown into a comfortable office. It was a long walk and I struggled to cope with the pain of getting there.

The man we had come to see was shown in and we had a chat. We both thought that he might be all right and agreed to give him a trial. He was delivered by a prison van the next day and it soon became clear that he really did know his stuff.

What a bit of luck it was for everybody concerned. We had thought that if he could manage some mucking out, filling hay nets, sweeping up and leading horses to and from the stables, he would be a terrific help.

In fact, he turned out to be a really gifted horseman, especially at getting young horses going.

His girlfriend, who had been driving down from London to see him at weekends while holding down a full weekday job, turned out to be a useful horsewoman. She came and stayed with us and between us all we got the business going again. I have deliberately not used his name as he is now a free man and working with horses. They have become real friends.

*

After this accident, we decided to use bigger, slower cobs as they might be more suitable for our novice customers.

I felt it might be wise to give myself an easier summer in order to recover a bit. We sold several young harness ponies and bought two more heavy cobs.

We also saw a modern waggonette that was for sale and bought it for a customer. It had been made in Poland and originally sold by Jonathan and Julian Talbot of Martock.

We went to see them and they let us have several Polish

We have taken part in several Western Counties Heavy Horse Workings with the Dales cobs. At one we used Mr Allen in a packhorse demonstration. We have also given carriage rides to the public. We don't have a lorry, so we can only take part if the workings are not too far away. It is so good that young people can see how it was all done only a few years ago. However, the future is also important and I can't see why working horses shouldn't play a large part in it.

I used to have a complete set of horse-drawn hay-making equipment. This consisted of a mower, old fashioned kicker hay turner, expanding hay rake (made by Huxtable in North Devon) a hay sweep and a hay pole, which is a type of crane worked by a horse to put the hay onto the rick.

As is quite usual, I needed some money, so they had to go. Chris Murray of Pennywell Farm offered me a good price for the lot. It is a visitor farm so now these rare implements can be seen by lots of people, and hopefully preserved for future generations.

I used the money to buy a pair of new wheels for our coach.

*

Since this chapter is all about my four-legged friends it seems the right moment to talk about dogs. I have always had dogs sharing my life. Sitting here thinking back I realise how many have come and gone, many of which I have forgotten, I'm ashamed to say.

My first doggie love was called Nell. She was a working terrier with the hunt and had a vicious reputation. It was generally believed that my Father was the only person who could handle her. I was only a toddler and had been told not to go near her. Well, of course, that was enough for me to want to cuddle up to her. I would sneak her into my bedroom at night and she slept on my bed, but as she was covered in fleas from going to ground after foxes, she left them everywhere. Mother was furious when she found out what I had been doing.

At that time there was a pack of foxhounds in a railed yard behind the kennels at Stiniel. I used to love to play with them, but soon learned that if I went into their yard they would knock me over, so I played with them through the rails.

I did my National Service in the Veterinary Corp where we all had to become dog trainers. I hated the guard dog training as we had to be so hard on the dogs, but I got on all right with tracking and mine dogs. I was issued with a demonstration dog called Hector, who was already trained.

After the Army I had a black lurcher, called Kips, with the idea that we could go rabbiting, but along came myxomatosis that killed all the rabbits. Kips took to killing chickens. He didn't take any notice of punishment; I doubt if he realised what he was being punished for, but somebody told me to put a muzzle on him and shut him in the hen run for a few weeks. I tried it and he never killed another chicken. He was with me for many years and was really quick. When Sally and I travelled down from Bristol to Devon in a gypsy caravan, Kips caught hares in the fields where we camped. He was the very devil for turning dustbins over.

Sally had two Shetland sheepdogs. One of them was very small. She had been kicked by a horse as a puppy. The vet thought that she wasn't going to come round after the anaesthetic, but to everybody's surprise she recovered, although she never grew any bigger.

In my haulage days I was driving a straw lorry early one morning when I saw a collie dog running about on the road at Siddington near Cirencester. When I returned home that night he was still there, so I thought that he might be lost. I called to him. He happily jumped into the cab and ate the rest of my sandwiches. I drove him home and rang Cirencester Police. They asked if I was prepared to look after him until somebody came looking. I called him Lost. He stayed with me for some six months and we became great mates.

One morning a man, who was clearly a farmer, came to claim him. I was more than a bit suspicious, but it was obvious from the way they greeted each other that Lost was his dog. He explained that he lived and farmed on the Mendips and had been driving from there to Hull in an open-back Landrover with the dog in the back. He didn't miss him until he arrived in Hull and he had no idea where the dog had jumped out. His wife was ill and died not long afterwards, so it was a while before he had had time to search properly. He had then re-traced his journey

49 Driving Badger & Mr Allen to the Exeter City coach
on Lammas Day, June 2007.

50 Badger & Dusty attending a wedding at the Two Bridges Hotel. October 2007.

51 Rose Gaisford and Carolyn Owen using Victoria
to bank potatoes, June 2008.

52 Gill Otway driving pony team Ben, Vodka, George & Annie,
June 2008.

53 Driving Padgent & Victoria, September 2008.

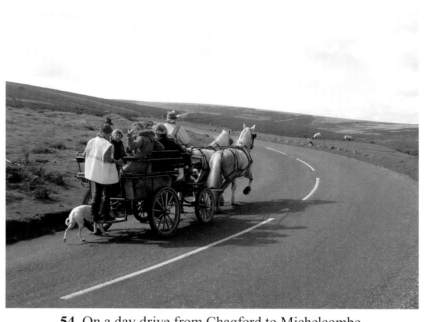

54 On a day drive from Chagford to Michelcombe.

55 A new pair of ponies bought, broken and trained for a client, winter 2008.

56 Instructing with Victoria on the trotting track at Michelcombe.

57 Driving Maddy, leaving Michelcombe.

58 The harness room at The Brookings.

59 An instruction session on full collars in the harness room at Michelcombe.

60 Tenner with new friend Nort 2001.

61 Tenner and Nort in the snow, 2009.

62 Ponies in the snow in the Knapp, winter 2009.

63 Carriage drive with Easdon Tor in the background.

64 Four generations of the Arden family.

calling at all the police stations along the way.

The sergeant in Cirencester remembered that I had found a dog, so they were happily re-united. I thought that was the end of the story, but many months later I was driving my lorry up Burrington Coombe on the Mendips when two collies jumped out onto the road. I instantly recognised Lost and called to him. He came straight back to me. I was able to give him a pat before sending him on his way.

I described earlier the occasion when Sally and I and the children spent days looking for a missing terrier called Trouble. We eventually found him when our whippet showed me where to dig. The whippet was called Blondie, because she never was very bright. She was killed when a large chicken house that Sally was taking down fell on her.

At about this time I was invited to visit a lady I knew. I was a bit nervous about going as I owed her for some hay that I couldn't afford to pay for. She invited me to stay for supper and then showed me a litter of collie puppies that she was desperate to get rid of. Having been softened up by the good supper and some whisky, I picked one out and took him home. I called him Tigger and he was to become one of the best running dogs that I ever had. He would go all day beside horses or a carriage and travelled hundreds of miles with me. He lived for about sixteen years and came with me to Michelcombe. He is buried in our dog graveyard here. What a pity they have to go so soon.

Soon after I moved to Stinhall I was given a corgi that didn't have much between the ears. I was taking a party trekking one day when a car pulled up. A door opened, the corgi jumped in, the car drove off and I never saw her again.

I've had a lot of Jack Russells over the years. One was called Mitch and he used to have such trouble when following our horses across the moor as he never seemed to be able to stick to any track and struggled with the long grass. He used to take it out on the sheep. It took a long time to break him of that habit. Unfortunately, he got run over while Maggie and I were on holiday.

Soon after this I saw an advertisement for some collie cross whippet puppies at Sigford. When I got there the owner told me that I could have the pick of the litter for five pounds. I picked the first one that showed himself. The owner protested that he had wanted to keep that one, but I insisted that I would have him and the owner gave way.

I called him Fiver, as that was what he had cost. He grew up to be the best running dog that I ever had. We were doing a lot of long distance journeys with the ponies at this time, but thirty or forty miles a day was nothing to him. He regarded himself as the king of the road. Any dog that ran out barking as we went past was quickly sorted out by Fiver. Lots of farm collies found themselves being bowled over.

An old gypsy who had known me all my life said to me that Fiver was just like I used to be. I asked him what he meant.

"He's always travelling, fighting and fond of the ladies." No Comment.

Even when he was a deaf old dog he hated being made to ride on the cart. It was below his dignity.

Freebie was a hairy lurcher puppy who came from Nicky Gaisford. He cost nothing, hence Freebie. He didn't have much brain, but was such a nice dog. In middle age he caught kennel cough, and when the vet checked him out he found that he also had a hole in his heart. It wasn't until much late in his life that it affected his running, but it cost a lot in vet's bills to keep him going. He looked like a small wolfhound. I had great fun one day winding up a silly girl who had a car covered in anti-hunting posters. I described to her in great detail how we farmers hunted the wolves on Dartmoor. She said that I was a cruel old man and anyway he looked a bit small to catch a wolf. I told her that the Dartmoor wolves were very small – and she believed me!

Coming from a hunting family I have walked a lot of hound puppies: by that I mean that I have looked after puppies for several months while they are growing into foxhounds. I usually had them two at a time.

One particular pair caused me a lot of expense and grief. The first one got run over by a customer and I had to have him put down. Soon after that unfortunate incident, the other puppy got kicked by a horse and broke his shoulder. I took him to the vet who had a young assistant who offered his services free as long as I paid for the drugs.

The puppy was operated on and his shoulder pinned. In order to restrict his movements in the early days after the operation it was necessary to confine him to a large corn bin. He was having doses of steroids and tranquillisers in order to keep him as still as possible. Eventually he was allowed to move to a loose box and then into a small yard. Amazingly, he became perfectly sound and grew into a very big hound – perhaps the steroids had something to do with this! He returned to the kennels in due course.

The following year he won the prize for the best working hound at the puppy show. It was only after this that I admitted to Bernard Parker, the huntsman, what had happened.

Sometime after moving to Michelcombe, my daughter Clare became the partner of Patrick Cooper who was then Master of the South Devon Hunt. I agreed to walk puppies for them. Nicky and Rose Gaisford were living in a caravan here at the time, so they were able to help a lot with these puppies. Thank goodness nothing terrible happened to any of them. I took two puppies each year for three years and I'm pleased to say that I can remember their names: they were Waxwing and Warrior; Candle and Cautious; Fancy and Fantasy. It was great fun having them around, but as I got busier every year with the driving I reached the stage when I couldn't take in any more.

This brings me up to the present day dogs, Tenner and Nort, both collies: their names again indicating what they cost.

Tenner came as a puppy from near South Zeal. He will never be as tough as Fiver, but he is a super dog. He has very successfully done obedience training at classes at Totnes. As a young dog he was very unlucky to be run over by a car and break a leg very badly. The vets in Totnes did a marvellous job on him and saved the leg. It cost a lot more than a tenner! He is nearly as good as new.

I saw an advert for an eight month old collie in the Free Ads paper – 'free to a good home'. Maggie rang up about him, and was told that some people in Bodmin were coming up to look at the dog that day, and she was sure they would have him. As Maggie was about to put the phone down she asked if she could leave her phone number in case they didn't want the dog. Two hours later the phone rang – they didn't want him, he was too boisterous. So Maggie and Neil (the dog trainer) went to look at him.

He was living in a small house with only a very small garden and, as the couple were old and infirm, he was getting almost no exercise – not a good thing for a strong young collie. But Maggie and Neil thought he would be OK for our life, so home he came and he gained the name, Nort. Luckily Tenner also approved of the new arrival and they soon became firm friends.

Nort soon settled down and loves this life, but has some hang-ups from his previous life: he is very frightened of the sound of gunshots; he doesn't like low flying jets and can be very frightened in strange circumstances. For example, he hates Maggie doing the ironing. On the other hand, when I ask him to clear cattle from a moorland road he can be quite aggressive and loves chasing them off. He has learned that he mustn't chase sheep and will run through a flock of sheep without taking any notice of them.

Nort has developed a party trick. When we are going up to Combestone Tor he tears off ahead, does a short cut off the road and waits for us at Venford car park, and then he does the same again at the Tor. I haven't the least idea how these tricks started. He's not as clever as Tenner, but he's a real nice chap, and very good-looking!

Nort and Tenner just love to have a good howling session. They do this to order, and even won a prize at a local dog show for it.

It's lovely to have animals with personality.

CHAPTER 14

The summer of 2008 and the winter that followed

We no longer make any hay ourselves as we are always too busy with the driving at haymaking time, so we have to buy it all in.

There was a very brief spell of nice weather in June. I saw an advert for some hay in round bales near Exeter. This sounded like just the job, so Maggie and I jumped into the car to go and have a look.

It started to pour with rain as we drove over there.

When we arrived at the farm we could see these round bales standing out in the rain. Our hearts fell, but the farmer took us up the rough muddy track to inspect the bales. We drove around the field and tested several at random. It was indeed some nice June hay.

We went home and asked John French's advice as to whether the bales would have been damaged by the rain.

He thought that the rain wouldn't have gone in too far. I rang the farmer and agreed to take as many bales as I could fit into our home made barns.

Next morning we made up a convoy of three 4x4s and trailers and set off to make hay in pouring rain. It was Carolyn's first attempt at towing a trailer. We kept on hauling hay all the weekend as fast as we could.

The weather was as bad as it could possibly be. When I was unloading some of the last of the bales the water was just running out of the bottom of them.

By now I thought that I had really dropped a clanger.

I pulled all the carriages and everything out of every shed in order that I could put the bales in the dry and leave room round them for the air to circulate.

Whenever we had a fine day, which wasn't very often, I used the fore end loader to move the bales out into the sun and wind in order to dry them out as much as possible.

Amazingly this crazy hay making seems to have worked as the hay is turning out very well. What would Father and all the old men say about this way of haymaking? Certainly no time to enjoy cream teas in the sun as we used to.

The awful weather continued all summer. It seemed to rain almost every day during July and August. We suffered a big drop in visitors: not good for the bank balance.

Worse was to come as the dreadful summer was followed by the toughest winter in the twenty years that we have lived here. We only had snow for a few days, but it was deep and very cold with it – it took me back to 1963. But these days we are much better equipped to deal the weather.

When the snow first hit it was blowing a real blizzard. We couldn't get any transport up to check our Knapp fields, so Maggie and Carolyn fought their way through the drifts (several feet deep) on foot to check the ponies. They were all well and still had enough hay. By the next day I was able to get up there with the tractor, a shovel at the ready in case I needed it. The rest of the winter was very cold with the ground frozen solid. We had to stop driving for several weeks and our winter bookings have been almost non-existent.

Following the bad summer, things were difficult. I had to look around for another way to earn a shilling.

I had been asked to look for a matched pair of pedigree Dartmoor Ponies, but I thought it an almost impossible task. I was asked to find them, buy them and break them to drive.

Years ago I had an order for some pedigree Dartmoors to go to New England. Maggie and I travelled all over England looking for them. We found ponies, but none of them matched.

I happened to see an advert in our local church magazine for a pedigree pony sale at Postbridge. I went along to the sale with almost no hope of finding what I wanted. I didn't take my cheque book or even a trailer to bring anything home. There were some forty ponies at this sale. I was having a look around when I saw two nice ponies in the same stable. I asked to have them taken out to see if they matched and had them trotted to see how they moved.

I could see that they were a real possibility.

I had to ring Maggie and ask her to bring the cheque book and trailer.

This pair are called Petrock and Piran after two Cornish saints. They had obviously been well handled and were willing to be caught and led around. That was a good start. With Carolyn, Rose and Nicky helping we soon got harness on them and got them lunging in the round corral. It wasn't long before we got them pulling a log around and indeed going on the trotting track beside Vodka, a very experienced home-bred Dartmoor pony. Sadly this was to be Vodka's last job.

Once the young Dartmoors were going OK and could go as a pair themselves, we turned Vodka away in the Knapp field for a winter holiday. He had been there for a few weeks when one day I wasn't very happy about the way he looked. I came home for the trailer, and Maggie and Carolyn came to help.

To my horror we could only just get him into the trailer; he seemed to have lost control of his back legs. I drove him home very carefully, and we managed to get him into a loose box, but by then it was obvious that he was beyond help. I rang Mike Weir of the Dartmoor Hunt, who kindly turned out late on a Sunday evening to put him down. A very sad end to a wonderful, loyal pony of about eighteen years that I had broken in and used in single, pair, teams, unicorn and also in my tandem of six. Such a nice honest pony. We will miss him.

Old friends Lee Bonnel and Cathy Hudlass came to see us and brought their young son, Cameron. Lee was able to give me some help with the pair of young Dartmoors. He's a good man to have around if I feel I may have some more difficult ponies. He is so quick to step in at times of emergency.

So we got Petrock and Piran out together as a pair on the road for the first time, and they went very well. A couple more weeks of driving and they were ready to go to their new home. Although they are a bit small they have been great fun to drive and have provided some useful winter income.

Lee had brought down with him a pony called Tommy for us to try. We put him in a pair with Carolyn's Ben. They went

215

away well, but as we were leaving Holne Tommy started to kick and managed to get his leg over the pole.

Although he kept kicking, he couldn't get it back. Meanwhile they were sailing up the hill. Lee turned them into the hedge. We grabbed heads and got Tommy out of the vehicle with a bit of puffing and struggling. Paula, who lives at Holne Court, saw what was happening and rushed out with a glass of whisky for me – very welcome! The pony was too frightened to just put him straight back in, so Lee rode him home bareback while I drove Ben on one side of the pole, just as I have seen in pictures of turnouts taken in Bulgaria and Hungary. I had never done this before with a pole and only one pony. It was rather a direct reminder of the loss of poor Vodka, Ben's former regular pair partner.

When we got home we put Tommy and Ben together again in a waggonette with a much higher pole and drove them on the trotting track successfully.

What a Sunday morning for this old pensioner.

*

The difficult winter really wasn't helped by being beset with tractor problems.

I managed to buy some hardcore to put down on the trotting track as the surface had got very muddy with all the use it had had. Just as I was finishing spreading it I managed to get the loader hooked up in a piece of scrap iron and broke a hydraulic pipe. Our tractor mechanic pointed out that the tractor was also due for a service.

We had a huge bill for the servicing and when we got the tractor back I could hear a strange noise coming from the engine. Our mechanic said that the water pump had gone wrong, but that it was all right to use the tractor to take bales out to the horses.

I was taking a bale up to the Knapp when there was an almighty bang from the engine. As we were blocking a narrow lane I had to drive the tractor the short distance home. The fan had broken up and the blade had gone through the radiator. I was more than a bit upset by this as we had been waiting for a fortnight for a new water pump. Many angry phone calls later we finally had the tractor back on the road just in time for the heaviest snow fall that we have had for years.

The track to the Knapp had some very deep snow drifts across it. I took the tractor up there and managed to clear the way. I was beginning to feel a bit better about this tractor as I drove home. I had to stop to open a gate. Maggie was in the yard. Just as I walked back to get into the tractor she shouted a warning and grabbed me as the tractor just took off on its own and ran into the hedge with a crash. I had been looking at Maggie and didn't hear anything as I had left the engine running so I was quite unaware of what was happening.

It only just missed me by inches. My guardian angel must still be with me in yet another escape.

I made up my mind instantly that we just had to sell this tractor even though I knew that we would make a real loss on it. I hope somebody else has better luck with it than I have.

*

I went up to Lisa James' and Paddy Hext's yard and bought a set of pony pair's harness. While I was there I saw a carriage trailer that they had for sale. I suddenly realised that it might be possible to move a round bale with this trailer as it was fitted with a winch and low to the ground, with ramps.

I made them an offer that they accepted. Carolyn and I have since used it to move a bale. We hooked it onto the back of a waggonette pulled by Padgent.

Horse power has won again!

Carolyn and I have just been to Exeter horse market where I spotted a very nice type of cobby pony that was for sale. Prices were very poor due to the present financial climate. I was able to buy him for less than £500. Rose is riding him in the round corral. He is very green, but I am sure he will make a nice pony one day. Rose lunged him today, put harness on him and pulled a log in the round corral. He will make a driving pony I am sure.

*

Although the media has made a great fuss about this spell of bad weather, it has not been a patch on some of the bad winters we had in the seventies, and certainly nothing like the hell we had to endure in 1963. But having deep snow again has reminded me of some past experiences in the snow, and this seems a good point to describe them.

On the way home one winter's night, I was leaving Exeter when the police stopped me and advised me not to go on. It was snowing, but they said it was much heavier up on the moor. As I had no money on me, I had to go on. I finally got stuck on Meldon Hill about two miles from home.

I got out and tried to scrape the snow away from the back wheels. As I was bending over something knocked me over. It was my own van sliding backwards. Luckily I managed to roll clear or I would have been trapped. It was unlikely that anybody else would come along that night. Just another lucky escape to add to the list.

The next morning we had some customers booked for driving. The yard had very deep snow all over it. I couldn't even open the loose box doors and the concrete garage that we used to store the carriages had collapsed overnight with the weight of snow on the roof. I was certain that nobody could possibly turn up, so I was having a proper breakfast before tackling the muddle.

As we sat there a voice called out, "Is there anybody there?"

I just couldn't believe it, but there were the customers. They'd managed to drive reasonably close and then walked the rest of the way.

I tried to rise to the occasion, but it was not easy. Later in the morning it came on to snow again, very heavily, and I suggested that it would be wise if I got them back to their car before they became really snowed in. I drove my mare Beauty down to their car. It was buried in snow and even when I had shovelled it clear, the car wouldn't move. I had to tie a rope from the cart to the car and get Beauty to pull it clear.

During those years in the seventies we had several hard winters. We had some horses running in fields at Moretonhampstead. A kind lady used to look after them for me and I kept a supply of hay in a shed there. One morning she rang to tell me she couldn't get near the shed as the snow was over the top of it. We rode over and decided to drive the horses home loose on the road. There was no possibility of meeting any cars as the snow had blocked all the roads. We rounded up the horses, but for some reason an old Dales mare took it into her head to jump her way down a row of council house gardens, but nobody spotted her.

We next met a council roadman who said we couldn't take them through the village. "Like hell we can't!" I shouted and cracked my whip behind them. He leapt out of the way and swore at me. I was well used to that. On the way home there is a cutting at the bottom of a hill. The snow had formed a spectacular high arch right across the road.

We had a heavy snowstorm on Dartmoor that caught out a group of Air Cadets who were training for the Duke of Edinburgh's Award.

The Dartmoor Rescue rang me to ask if I would provide horses for a search party to ride out over the moor. I agreed on condition that I went with them to make sure that my horses were safe. I also knew very well the area of the moor that they wanted to search.

Off we went. They had brought a radio with them: a big cumbersome thing (no mobile phones then) and the radio operator was the least able rider. I had put him on Beauty, who was unlikely to get upset. Even she didn't like the funny noises that came from the radio. It turned out to be a waste of time anyway, as it didn't ever work.

The snow was drifting in the strong wind. We fought our way up the Lakeland valley to the *Warren House Inn*, which is one of the highest pubs in England. A policeman was on duty there. What he was supposed to do, I couldn't start to guess. We passed Caroline Bog, leaving it on our left – get into that one and you've had it – on over White Ridge to Grey Wethers and down to Teignhead farm, long since deserted. There is a small wood behind the farmhouse. I thought that the cadets might be sheltering there, but we couldn't find anybody. We had to retrace our tracks, as the area in front of us was very boggy.

The snow was blowing so hard that we couldn't see the

tracks we had just made. I suppose that the poor visibility precluded the use of helicopters. As it was getting dark we had to abandon our search. The only other people we saw were some soldiers with a Landrover at the edge of Fernworthy forest.

When we got home that night the television reported that hundreds of people were out searching the moor. Fortunately, the Cadets were found safe and well the next day.

On another occasion I was using Beauty to pull a sledge taking hay to some outlying ponies. The snow was quite deep. I met a farmer driving his Range Rover. He lent out of the window and told me that he was going home to tell his sons about me. They had been trying to start the diesel tractors on his farm that morning without much success.

Liz was bringing home some horses in the lorry when she got well and truly stuck in the snow. She had to abandon the lorry, but managed to get the horses out and into an old stable. There was no fodder there, so she rang me for help. I went outside, but my old van wouldn't start. Even if it had, I wasn't sure how close to the lorry I'd be able to get.

I had a Dartmoor pony that I had just broken to harness. I put him to a little exercise cart, put as much hay and straw on as I could and set off into the dark and snow. When I reached Chagford I was trotting up New Street when I saw some old Chagford men walking up the middle of the street. They never heard me coming so I got right up close behind them and then gave a loud shout. Didn't they jump!

I duly reached the stables where Liz and the horses were sheltering. We made the horses comfortable for the night and set out for home. As we crossed Rushford Bridge the sky cleared and the moon shone brightly on the snow. We could hear the church bells. A romantic scene if ever I saw one – but it was bitterly cold.

The manager of *The Manor House Hotel,* at that time run by British Rail (and known by the local railway staff as *Baskerville Hall*) rang me to ask if I was game to play a little game with some of the senior executives.

A chauffeur-driven car was picking up two executives and their wives from Exeter station. His idea was to arrange for the car to appear to break down and for me to come along with a carriage and offer them a lift.

So we set up the plan and agreed where the car would stop – a spot several miles from the hotel.

But the train was very late. It was terribly cold and snow started falling heavily. The car eventually appeared and stopped. I set off down the road to offer them a lift, which they gratefully accepted. Of course, they were not dressed for a winter night drive outside in the snow. Just as we reached the hotel the car caught us up. Only then did they begin to think they had been conned. I'm not sure what they really thought of being frozen.

I had to drive home using real trap lamps. They don't give much light.

CHAPTER 15

Family and Friends

As this book has really been a series of memoirs concentrating on my involvement with horses and haulage, I haven't spent much time talking about my family – and I expect they're all very relieved. But I would like to tidy things up a bit with a few words about my children.

I don't think I've mentioned Stephen, the eldest of my three children, since saying that he spent a year working on a farm before going to Bicton College. Although Stephen learned to ride, as did his sisters, unlike them he never really enjoyed it and I was happy for him to follow his own interests. After completing his course at Bicton, he went to Australia to get further farming experience, and then took over managing a dairy farm in deepest Wales – something of a challenge. Maggie and I visited him there and we were both impressed with the well-being of his cows in such a harsh environment.

While there, he met and married Maggie (another Maggie!), and they have a son, Ian. This farm was later sold, and they moved to another farm in Somerset, but farming was heading for hard times. Stephen decided it was time for a change and he now works for British Oxygen.

Ian has a degree in civil engineering from Cardiff university, and now lives in Sussex with his partner.

Honor, my middle child, learned to ride while still very young and soon started competing in show jumping. I described her competing at Prestbury when she was tiny. After moving to Stinhall, I devoted most of my time helping the girls with ponies, pony club and hunting – anything to take their minds off the death of their mother. Honor later rode some point-to-point horses for Mrs Brackenbury.

I last mentioned her when I said that she left business college in Exeter and went to live with Paddy Gallagher. Paddy has since died. They had a son, James. Honor now lives in Shropshire and works in a care home.

One winter's evening Maggie and I heard the sound of a powerful tractor pulling up outside Brookings. The door bell rang, and there was James. He was back in Devon and working on a local farm. He had borrowed the farmer's tractor to come to say hello to his grandfather. Since then we frequently see him and his partner, Emma. They live near Moretonhampstead. Emma is a teacher; James is successfully rearing pigs and doing stonewalling and hedge-laying.

Clare is my youngest daughter and, like Honor, always loved horses. She was only three when her mother, Sally, was killed in the tractor accident. At Stinhall Clare became friends with Peggy Harris and they had lots of fun riding on the moor together. She also was a keen member of the Pony Club and went hunting and to gymkhanas.

While Clare was still at South Devon College in Ashburton, she helped Jimmy Frost at his racing stables, only a few miles from here. When she left school I arranged for her to go to work at Jim Old's racing stables near Bristol. She got on well there and stayed for several years before coming back to Devon to work for Mr and Mrs Ogle, near Buckfastleigh. She ran their private yard of hunters and point-to-point horses. While there she met Patrick Cooper, who was Master of the South Devon Hounds and they have been together ever since.

Clare left the Ogle's to work with the South Devon at their kennels at Denbury.

Patrick later took over the Mastership of the West Percy hunt in Northumberland, where they worked for several seasons before moving back to Devon.

My sister, Norah, was always known as Tacker by the family. Tacker was ten years older than me, so sadly, we never really got to know each other very well. During the war she was a despatch rider in London with the ATS. Afterwards, she moved to Harpenden where she married Charlie Cockman. They both later worked for Brigadier Rayner at Ashcombe Towers. After Charlie's death, Tacker moved to Broadclyst in Devon, where she died a few years ago. We went to her funeral where, much to my surprise, there was a superb horse-drawn hearse with a pair of black Frisian horses. At the funeral I met Tacker's daughter, Maureen, for the first time since she was about fifteen.

While doing some research for me for this book, Carolyn found on the internet a message from Karen Piangnee, who wanted information on the Arden family. We duly rang her up and arranged to meet here.

It turned out that Karen is the daughter of Maureen and they both came, bringing with them Karen's baby, Grace – who is my great-great-niece.

What a meeting! It was lovely to have the chance to talk to Maureen again.

How good to have made contact with a whole new branch of the family.

*

Many people have helped me along the way, either in my personal life or in business. Sadly, some of them have passed away, but this is my chance to thank them all. My memory leaves a bit to be desired these days and I have no doubt left some good people out. I hope that those that I have failed to mention won't be too offended.

I'll start the list by going back to the early days

Gordon Bunch	whose father, Tom, was Father's kennel huntsman. Always known as Bunchy he was like a brother to me during my childhood. We played and fought together for many years. Sadly Bunchy and I have lost touch with each other. If you're reading this, Bunchy, please give me a ring.

Margaret Morcom	was helping me with my point-to-point horses during the year that I broke my jaw. She was such a nice girl. She sadly died from heart troubles when still quite young.
Dorothy, Liz, Sally and Sue	early girlfriends when we were so very young.
Ken Boulton	a professional steeplechase jockey who was in the Army with me. He was later killed at Uttoxeter races. We had been great mates and got into so many scrapes together.
David Hughes	was also a mate during Army days.

Moving on to Somerford times

Tamsin Butt	who became more like an adopted daughter and really seems like one of the family.
Derek Caswell	ex-apprentice jockey, who was involved with so many of my early doings at Somerford including flapping racing and hunting. Derek was also involved with us at Cheltenham.

Moving on to Stinhall

Liz	who bravely came to my aid at the most difficult time. Sadly, our marriage didn't work out, but I will always be grateful to her.
The late Arthur Palmer	who taught me to shoe horses originally and, many years later, helped me to start shoeing again at Stinhall.
Jack Sprague	who kindly offered me and my family joint use of Stinhall during the bad times.

Margaret Andrews	who so kindly looked after my daughters, Honor and Clare, after Sally was killed and I was trying to sort things out in Cheltenham.
Peggy Harris	Sam Harris's daughter. Childhood friend of Clare. I taught her to ride and she went on to compete in hunter trials. Peggy has recently written in a Dartmoor magazine about what the two of them got up to. It was a good job for them that I didn't find out then what it was!
Nigel and Margaret Mainwaring	who became very good friends.
Tona Cruickshank	a very glamorous blonde young lady, just out of school, who gave me terrific help in Stinhall days. Her mother and I were in the Pony Club together as children. Tona later trained as a veterinary nurse.
Mrs Dionne Leaman	who again helped a lot at Stinhall.
Ina and Wilhelm	a Dutch couple who ran a guest house at Murchington. They kindly sent us a lot of customers and they took me to Holland.
Mick McGlyn	a local farmer who gave me such a lot of help during some of these difficult times.
Lisa	who provided useful help for a season.
Bernard Parker	the huntsman of the Mid Devon Hunt at this time.

Gerald Adcock	who sold me Beauty, who was the mainstay horse of my early instruction days. His wife helped look after horses that I kept in fields at Moretonhampstead.
Chubb	a Glaswegian hippy girl who really helped me at the time I had my heart attack. I remember teaching her about planting a garden. Although of unusual appearance, and usually wearing hob-nailed boots, she was a very kind-hearted girl.
Howard Garbett	who came on the first driving course that I ever did. He lives just a few miles away now, and we see him quite often.

Finally, at Michelcombe

Peter Dodd	a real stalwart over all the time I have been here. He started here in the very early days and has worked for us for almost every Saturday ever since. He has helped with building the stables, coach house and barns. He has erected miles of post and rail fencing and helped me with all the heavy jobs. Peter's wife, Barbara, has helped Maggie for many years in the house.
Eloise Coombs	who helped us for several years before moving to Cornwall and then to France.
Nicky Bragg	helped in the early days at Michelcombe. She was still a school girl when she started and she learned to drive a four-in-hand before she was fifteen. She was a great girl. Nicky left us to become a children's nanny.

Lyn	who helped here before she left to start her own business in Cornwall. I still see her from time to time at Exeter horse market.
Nicky Gaisford	has been a helper over many years. She lived here in a caravan after her house caught fire. I look upon her daughter Rose as another adopted daughter. I taught her to ride and she used to come hunting with me. She has been away, but is now back helping again with young ponies.
Mike Oborn	helped here for several years. He helped in the construction of the wedding landau and the coach, and we did a lot of improvements to the stables.
Vida Alexander	helped us for several years and was very enthusiastic with the pony team.
Carolyn Owen	used to be a regular customer, but then decided on a complete change of occupation and left her I.T. job to help us here. Not only is she now our main helper with the horses, but she is also great on the maintenance front. Carolyn will turn her hand to anything from computers to plumbing.
The Ogle family	who gave me a lot of help in the early days at Michelcombe. Debora kindly moved my horses from Stinhall when I was at my wits end. Very sadly Michael, and his wife Pat, were killed while trying to cross on foot the A38 at Dean.

Mark Partridge	our farrier. I helped him to get his first customers when he qualified, and he has been coming here ever since. He always turns up on time, and does a "proper job". When I was shoeing my own horses he was always quite happy to come and help out occasionally if I ran out of time.
Robby Richardson	for his technical advice and help with shoeing problems.
John French	who sold me The Brookings, and later some land. Also for his help with moving big bales these days.
Michael French	for renting me the Knapp fields.
Judy Henderson	for grass keep.
Lee Bonnell and Cathy Hudlas	who gave us so much help after I broke my leg.

We have always been very fortunate in finding wonderful retirement homes for our horses and ponies. It's always sad to see them leave here, but at the same time it is very good to know that they will be so well cared for in their old age. So it's a big thank you to all those people.

Thanks to everyone in Michelcombe and Holne, who show such consideration to us and our horses on the roads about their homes.

And, of course, thanks to all the hundreds of customers over the years who have helped *Dartmoor Driving* to survive – long may they keep coming back!

Most important of all is Maggie, the mainstay of my life, and to whom I owe the most thanks. She came on the last course at Stinhall and later asked to come on another course.

Eventually, she was brave (or foolish) enough to transfer her job with B.T. from Kingston-upon-Thames to Exeter and joined me. We got married and are still together after more than twenty years.

Long may it last!

CHAPTER 16

In conclusion

I have attempted to remember and set down the more interesting things that have happened in my life, mainly with regard to a lifelong involvement with horses. That's all in the past. I feel that we should remember the past as it holds lessons to be learned.

But it is the present that is the most important, as it is what we have. The past has gone, and the future is all guesswork.

Just trying to earn a living has been, and still is, what mainly occupies me, but life must be fun as we only get the one shot at getting it right.

As a friend said to me, "The man who never risked making a mistake, never went anywhere."

No matter what troubles life throws at us, nothing can take away all the fun we have had. The nice memories from the fun times are with us for evermore.

Thank goodness we never know what lies in wait around the corner. I just go from day to day hoping to keep going as long as possible. Occasionally, trying to teach a particular client seems just a waste of time, even though I earn money from doing so. On the other hand it can be so rewarding when a pupil comes good.

It seems to me that with the ever increasing cost of oil, driving horses may well again become a useful form of transport. There are more people driving horses nowadays than for many years, certainly since the early 1930s.

Many years ago, when I first started teaching, an old gypsy asked me if I thought there was some long term significance in the increase in people wishing to learn to drive horses. At that time, almost everybody had long since given up horse-drawn transport. Perhaps he, like some of his people, could foresee the future.

There has lately been a tremendous amount of development in carriage-building, mostly because of the need for safe competition carriages. We now see hydraulic disc brakes, pneumatic tyres, easily adjusted shafts and poles and the use of non-traditional materials in the construction of carriages. Efficient brakes mean that horses no longer have to hold the cart back going downhill, which in turn means that horses can safely do an extended walk or even jog down hills. I have found that it is not a good idea to do a fast trot downhill, as it may well cause lameness.

I have had electric indicators and lights fitted to my working carts for safety, as modern motorists do not understand or recognise hand signals, let alone whip signals. I most certainly don't advise driving after dark unless well escorted but, as happened only today, the fog can come down very quickly on the moor. I was certainly glad to have lights today. With the days in winter it is very easy to run out of daylight when trying to get home late in the afternoon. The lights have also proved useful when passing through a wooded area where visibility is poor, even in summer, when driving under the shade of trees.

The use of high visibility clothing is most important as it may well give motorists that extra bit of time to see us.

I am no engineer, but I can see that if small engines of some sort were fitted to carriages to help up steep hills, it would make life much easier for the horse. Electric engines could be powered by batteries re-charged while driving on the flat or downhill. Perhaps the power could even be pedal power, as in bicycles.

A small engine, such as used on lawn mowers and chain saws could also be used to assist with going uphill. The Amish people use horse-drawn farm implements where the horse just moves the unit, but an engine powers the farm implements.

I have experimented with having a chain saw started up and run behind a pair of my horses and, quite surprisingly, they soon became used to the noise. With a bit of careful training they didn't even mind when the saw was revved up. By assisting the

234

horse in these ways journey times could be very much improved.

I have no doubt that the use of horses on farms will soon be on the increase. For use as transport it would be easy to improve upon weather protection. Of course we have lost the places, such as inns, in the towns and villages where we could safely leave our horses to be fed and sheltered. This doesn't mean that such places couldn't be found again.

Special roads built for horses could be seen alongside bicycle lanes within the next twenty or thirty years.

Life for me seems to be just rushing past. But at least I like to think that all the adventures, hard work and clangers dropped in this second half of my life may prove to be of use to my fellow man.

The art and craft of carriage driving and working horses on the land had very nearly been lost when, for some reason beyond my understanding at the time, the good Lord sent me along the path of teaching driving and training horses to go in harness. I have been lucky to have spent so many years teaching driving and working horses for all sorts of tasks. I just love being out over Dartmoor, driving my horses and passing on my knowledge of both driving and of the history and customs of Dartmoor.

Along the way, Maggie and I have provided homes and a good life for so many horses and Dartmoor ponies who otherwise might have wound up on the horse meat scrap yard.

We have also been able to provide employment and training for a lot of grooms and income for our farrier, vets, garages, farmers and merchants.

And I have attempted to re-introduce the Devon Packhorse, an ancient breed, using a homebred Morgan stallion.

The foot-and-mouth outbreak indirectly led me to write that first little story that was published in *Carriage Driving Magazine*. Since then the same magazine has published a lot of my anecdotes. This obliged me to learn to type. And the end result of that is this book, in which I hope you have found something of interest.

Don't forget – if there's anything in this book that you fancy having a yarn about, you know where to find me.

DARTMOOR DRIVING

JOHN AND MAGGIE ARDEN
THE BROOKINGS
MICHELCOMBE
HOLNE, ASHBURTON
DEVON, TQ13 7SP
Tel: 01364 631438
www.dartmoordriving.btinternet.co.uk

DARTMOOR DRIVING is a small family business, established in 1977, with the aim to widen your carriage driving experience, and at the same time give you a holiday.
The complete beginner is as welcome as the experienced driver.
We offer many different types of driving holidays, with or without accommodation.

CARRIAGE DRIVING INSTRUCTION
John is fully qualified to instruct you in all aspects of carriage driving, including singles, pairs, tandem & team; either just for fun or more seriously. Although we do not now take horses for training to harness, we can offer practical advice to help you get your horse going at home. We have a wide range of driving equipment to show you.

INTRODUCTION TO DRIVING
A taster session for those who are completely new to carriage driving, briefly covering as many aspects as we can, including a drive out. This can either be a half day or an hour and a half session. Ideal for newcomers to see if carriage driving is for them.

HOLIDAY DRIVES
A morning's drive to Combestone Tor, for those who would like to be taken for a drive out with the horses. John will enthral you with his knowledge of Dartmoor life, both past and present, as you savour the atmosphere at the gentle pace of the horses.

FULL DAY MOORLAND DRIVES
A day to remember! Join us at The Brookings and we transport a pair of horses, carriage and people across Dartmoor to The Duke of Windsor car park near Chagford. From there we drive back along quiet country lanes, unused by most visitors, stopping for lunch either at a pub or with a picnic by the Wallabrook. On through Spitchwick estate to Newbridge and back home. Whether you want to share the driving of the horses or just sit back and relax, this is a unique way to enjoy Dartmoor.

ACCOMMODATION
We have twin-bedded en-suite accommodation, with the option of all meals with us.

GIFT VOUCHERS
Available for a full day, a half day or for a specific value, they are valid for 6 months.

****

IF YOU HAVE ANY QUERIES, PLEASE RING US, AND WE HOPE TO SEE YOU SOON
AT DARTMOOR DRIVING.

LOOKING FOR A BOOK THAT'S OUT OF THE ORDINARY?

SEE OUR CURRENT LIST OF TITLES AT
www.moorhenpublishing.co.uk

ARE YOU WRITING A BOOK?
Manuscript appraisals: an independent assessment
will provide valuable guidance.

Proofreading: polish your manuscript by having it
professionally proofread.

Contact us at mail@moorhenpublishing.co.uk
or by telephone on 01803 856449

HAVE YOU SELF-PUBLISHED A BOOK?
Successful marketing requires reviews.
Our Book Review Service will help.
Find the link on www.moorhenpublishing.co.uk